REAL MEN DON'T
NEED CLOSETS

Revealing and Dealing with Unknown Marriage Secrets

T. Charles Brantley

Outskirts Press, Inc.
Denver, Colorado

By Timothy C. Brantley
Pastor of Restoration Springs Inter-denominational Church
1575 Thomaston Avenue
Waterbury, CT 06704
203-753-7377
www.rest.org

REAL MEN DON'T NEED CLOSETS
Revealing and Dealing with Unknown Marriage Secrets

Outskirts Press, Inc.
http://www.outskirtspress.com

ISBN: 978-1-4327-1252-5

Outskirts Press and the "OP" logo are trademarks belonging to Outskirts Press, Inc.

PRINTED IN THE UNITED STATES OF AMERICA

THIS BOOK IS WRITTEN
FOR CHRISTIANS AND NON-CHRISTIANS
. . . So Drop Your Stones

This book is dedicated to my wife of more than twenty years, Jackie Brantley. In addition to God in Christ, she is an important aspect of my life. Through her CONSTANT love and patience, the relationship has endured the good, bad, and ugly.

Thanks to my children, Timothy Charles Brantley II and Jocelyn Racquel Brantley, whom I know and pray will supersede me in every aspect of their lives.

This book is for both Christian and non-Christian couples. The points can be applied to both couples. However, Christian couples, be warned, going to church and making Christ your savior is not enough to survive a marriage; it takes work.

For non-Christian couples, I believe if you need God for the wedding ceremony, you need him throughout the marriage. When non-Christian couples have struggles between them, who is the best person to call? I believe the answer is Jesus the Christ.

If you do not know Jesus the Christ, I encourage you to accept him as Lord and savior, and find a church home to mature your relationship.

Contents

Introduction

I have to confess that I have not read the books on "Down Low Men" (married men who have sex with men and women), because I cannot understand how a man can treat his wife that way and still say he loves her. Yet this book does not condemn a brother for the sin of homosexuality. The Bible says it is a sin, with which I agree. In respect, this book will hopefully persuade a brother to be truthful with himself, God, and the woman he loves. Judgment of eternity is not mine to give, but God's. Yet, the judgment of self and how he treats his wife is something that may be dealt with within one's lifetime. I pray brothers who are on the Down Low will finally get on the Up High.

Remember this point throughout this book: a woman loves truth. A wife would rather know her husband's hurt versus a man who lies about a hurt. A wife would rather know her husband's sexual tendencies versus finding them out through the grapevine or a STD test. In addition, any doctor will tell you that a wound that is covered and not treated will eventually lead to more pain down the road. Brothers, your secret may be horrible. Your secret may be ugly, hurtful, and downright sinful, BUT you still must tell the truth. In this book, we will reveal how MEN should uncover all sexual sins to their wives.

On one hand, I feel homosexuals have been beat up. This is not my assignment for this book. We have preached against it, yet I have not heard compassion in our voices. I believe the sin to be dealt is admitting his guilt not just to God, but also to his wife. This is the main point of this book. I am talking about freedom. This is only done through truth.

It is not just being free from people; it's being free from yourself. Even if you are in the sin of being down low, the honorable thing you can do is live the truth instead of a lie. A non-truthful man has hurt a woman who may be reading this book. Why continue a lying spirit to your family concerning your sexuality or unknown sexual passions? Many secular people will debate about sexual orientation, but all agree that lying is wrong. Upon that, stop doing it, especially in the black community. The top 10 deaths for 40 and over white females do not include HIV. Yet if you look at the 40 and over black female top 10 deaths, you will see HIV deaths. Why? Because some black men will not speak the truth.

The following proves my above statement from the National Vital Statistics Reports Volume 55, No. 10 dated March 15, 2007. The information is based on 2003 data.

Black female Age	Ranking of HIV caused death
20-24 years	4
25-34 years	3
35-44 years	3
45-54 years	4

For the same age breakout, black male ranking of HIV causing death was 6, 4, 2, and 3, respectively. The numbers are too shocking to believe. I know people may say the deaths are due to drug use, yet my point remains: if more men would speak the truth of their sexual orientation or secrets, these numbers among women would decline.

Adam hid from his sin. Man has not changed. Yet throughout this book, I pray you will turn things around in your life by being honest about yourself to your wife. Honesty is truly the best policy as it relates to life. This book is not just for men on the "down low"; it is for men who need to come clean with their wives on a day-in and day-out basis about everything, especially their sexual tendencies.

Chapter 1:
Truth and Lying

Back in the early 1300s through 1600s, men were known for having something called valor. Valor is a big word for bravery. Due to societal changes, such things are not called upon. However, I believe the new form of valor is called truth. When a man can tell the truth even if it hurts, he has valor.

The first point to start with is our sexuality. If a man can reach down to the bottom of his tormented soul and tell the truth, even when it deals with his sexuality, he has truly become a man of valor. Remember when Abraham sent his servant, Eliezer, to find a bride for his son

Isaac? Abraham made a vow with Eliezer by touching his thigh (Genesis 24:2). In addition, Acts 16:3 implies that Paul circumcised Timothy. Such points are not without analysis.

Meaning when men become truthful from the loins up, everything else will become easy to speak, too. I hear Christians who say this does not count, but it does matter. Men's prized possessions are their loins, so when a man can speak truth from his loins, he will be able to speak truth from other parts. Yes, it starts in the heart of truth. When a man is not honest with God and his wife, truth will be hampered.

In antiquity, men of valor knew there was a fifty percent chance that they might not come back home, but they went anyway. Can we find men today who will march into the lives of their loved ones and tell the truth even if this means the death of a relationship? Such men will die in truth instead of a lie. Many men are living with a lie as they make love to their wives. Such will ultimately kill the relationship. Men must be men of standard—not just in public, but also, more importantly, in private.

Men, our wives long for a relationship. One that is not full of lies and espionage, but truth in the heart and loins. Yes, the truth of God must first be in our hearts and then flow through our extremities, especially our loins. When a man becomes converted through the grace of Jesus the Christ, he should become honest enough to tell his wife everything. In speaking the truth, you establish a great line of communication.

Men need sex to relate. Women need truthful communication to relate. Men, even if it hurts, she wants the truth. Many men walk around with the pain of not showing their wives their identity. It is like your wife being married to Superman and she does not know it. Today, my brother, take a deep breath and begin to tell her truth. Yes, even the dirty truth about yourself.

Living in the truth is much stronger and healthier. When you are in truth, no one can un-mask you because the ones closest to you already know you. I remember the wrestling of old, when I was a child, and there were always the people who wore masks. And many times when the fight started, the opponent of the masked person would go for the disguise. The masked man would forget his wrestling skills and immediate protect his mask (identity).

I see many men doing the same today. Instead of being naked before their wives, men put masks on, and every time their wives try to de-mask them, the defense mechanisms come up.

Something has to change to correct this problem. Lois Lane did not want Superman; she really wanted Clark Kent. The same is said for you, my brother. Your wife does not want a preacher, politician, or great man when you come home; she really wants you. Walk in the light, and you will not be a child of darkness. Be upfront with your woman. Be a man of valor and be strong enough to admit your weakness, sexual exploits, and, most importantly, your orientation.

Hear me on this one, brother. I am not saying go on a loud speaker and tell the world your secret. In fact, when your wife knows something about you that no one else knows, it makes her feel special. Why? Because now she is guarding your secret if she so chooses.

She is your covering brother. Just ask Sarah. Twice, she was asked by Abraham to lie for him. And she did. Again, tell your wife first and alone.

Ask yourself, am I strong enough to admit my weakness to my wife? This takes a true man. Because a great man of valor needs protection, not just when it comes to his strengths, but especially his weaknesses. If a man can confess to his wife, he can confess to the world. Men, we have our marching orders. Our women and children depend on us to fight the good fight of faith in truth.

Genesis 3:10 - "And he said, I heard thy voice in the garden, and I was afraid, because I was naked; and I hid myself." Men do not want to live in truth, because this is what Adam did. And his misdeed has passed down from generation to generation. My brothers, uncover your mask. Let her see your identity. In reality, she knows it already.

Be a true man of valor today.

Chapter 2:
Covering Up Is Not
the Right Thing to Do

It is one thing to have sin; it is another to cover it up from the wife of your union. This, in my mind, is unacceptable. Having or committing sin is nothing new. In fact, the Bible says that all have sinned and come short of the glory of God. We got this nature of sinning from our father Adam.

Yet one thing that we can change from our father Adam is the cover-up. You remember in the Bible how Adam ran when he heard God coming in the cool of the day. And Adam hid because of the nakedness.

Before we dive into this section, does it not make you wonder why God came in the cool instead of the heat of the day? And by God knowing all, He could have come in fire, but He came in cool. Yes, our God is cool.

In my humble opinion, we have a God that knows our faults, yet He still comes to us. Have you ever wondered why God did not strike us down in the very hour of our sin? He, coming in the cool, gives the answer in Genesis. Thank God, He comes in the cool and not in the heat. Do not get me wrong. There is a side of God that is hot and quick to judgment. Yet for the most part, He shows us the cool rather than the hot for those who sincerely love and appreciate Him. He comes to the cool for those who confess their faults and understand we are all saved by His grace.

I am trying to stress the importance of not covering up your sin, brothers. We all are sinners and will continue until Jesus comes back. The only covering we have is the covering and redeeming feature of Jesus the Christ. Therefore, when a man is on the down low, he is guilty of not only sinning with homosexuality but also covering up his sin. This is not the will of God. Hiding ANY sexual secrets from your wife in my mind is sin.

If God came to Adam and Eve in the cool, He

will do the same for you. Hiding your sin is making the sin an abomination. In other words, you are making the wound of sin bigger. You cannot hide garbage, because the smell will give it away. I say the same for men on the down low. I say the same to men who are not speaking the truth to their wives.

Again, I must always use grace in my book, because I believe Jesus the Christ is the essence of Mercy and Grace. We all have sinned and come short of the glory of God. I cannot stand here and offer myself as a pure and perfect example of holiness, because I am not. I can only offer up the power of confession and not covering up something that your wife knows already.

Many men may say that their wives do not know, but I beg to differ. Yes, she may not comment, but because she does not comment does not mean she does not know what is going on in and through your life. In essence, all I am saying to you who are married is that if you are finding yourself in a sin, it is time to come clean to your wife. May this book serve as the icebreaker so that you and your wife can finally put things out in the open.

And yes, I know the results may not be in your favor, brother, because you still lied for all those years. And yes, there may be a punishment up to divorce that you may have to endure. However, isn't it better to walk in the light than in the dark? In the dark, you keep hitting things, while in the light you see things more clearly.

You are a man. Paul said, "When I become a man, I put away childless things." One thing a child does is play "Hide and Seek." You are no longer a child, my brother; you are a man who needs to handle his business correctly, continually, and truthfully.

Throughout this book, you will hear the word "truth." It is because for too long men have lived in lies. The hardest thing for men to do is speak the truth. I know there may be brothers who say, "What about my wife?" This book is about men. And, in reality, brothers, if you live it, your wife will follow. Remember the quote: "If you build it, they will come"? Well, brothers, if you speak the truth, your respective wives will follow correctly.

In our minds, we would rather think what we are going to say when our wives confront us. This is the groundbreaking for a lie. Truth does not need rehearsals. Truth can stand on its own. Even again, if your wife leaves you, at least you can say she left for the truth's sake and not lies.

What a powerful revelation that all across America, a wife would say, "I left my husband because he told me the truth," rather than, "I found out the truth." Men, I know this is deep and hard at times to do, but we have to make that change. Change not for change's sake, but for the sake of our families.

Stop the hiding and move toward the light within and without of your life. Do not be easily shaken or turned by what you see and what you have become through lies. Uncover and let the wound of your heart begin to heal. Furthermore, when you cover, you pass on diseases as well.

In many cultures, heirlooms are passed down from generation to generation. Well, men, we do not have heirlooms, but we have certain characteristics we can give to someone else. And whether you know it or not, you are passing something down to the next generation. When you continue to lie, cheat, and steal, you pass this down to the next generation. When you come home and are faithful to your family, you pass this down to another generation.

Oh, the earth shakes for men who will live in truth and not in lies. As men pass down heart disease, let us pass down something greater in life that will change lives and not destroy them:

the heritage of telling the truth.

They say the highest increases in STDs are among the middle-aged. I feel this has happened because of the many cover-ups men have had in the past. Walk in the light, my brothers.

Chapter 3:
Why Are You in Secret About It

If a man does not want his wife to have a secret, why does he? Respect is a powerful word in a relationship. If the man wants all the information about his wife, he should do the same for her as well. Therefore, the question is, why have a secret? There should be no secrets.

There are many secret societies where men divulge their innermost secrets to other men. But last I read in the Bible, it said that when a man and woman become married, they become one. The same holds if there are secret societies among spouses. That is, if a man is living on the down low, he needs to confess to his wife. You must understand that down low activity is not just homosexuality, but adultery. It amazes me that no one has tackled the point.

When a man who is married steps out with anyone besides his wife, that is the sin of adultery. You may disagree with me on the sin of homosexuality, but you cannot when it comes to adultery. No one wants to be played or placed in such an arena. For the secular, the word homosexuality is not wrong, with which I disagree. Yet the secular world agrees together that adultery (lying) is wrong in any shape and fashion.

Sometimes I think people split hairs on issues that affect a nation. One common denominator of the pain within our society is the erosion of family. And, in many cases, the reason for the erosion is adultery. Whether you have sex with a different sex or same sex, it is still adultery. Men or women on the down low are not excluded from the category of adultery. They have taken their vow of love and devotion, and blown it into the wind. Such is causing a wider gap to solving the problem of family in America. So, hear me loud and clear. Down low is adultery.

There is something about the laws of God that

says you will reap what you have sown. What goes around will come around. If you do somebody wrong, somebody will turn around and do you wrong as well. This is the law of God. In essence, every man who is honest can say that he has felt that law in one way or another. If you do not communicate, it will come back on you. If you do not give good sex to your wife, it will come back on you. If you have secrets from your wife, it will come back on you repeatedly and again.

For men who are reading this book, I implore and encourage you to stop the madness and tell your wife the truth. As stated, this book is for whatever secret you may have. It is time to spill all the beans. If you really value life, you will value the importance of truth. I know the truth is ugly more times than pretty, but such things must be shared, especially when it comes to a wife and those closest to you. If you are on the down low when you sleep with your wife, you are passing on potential harmful STDs to your wife. In essence, your secret cannot remain one until the very end.

Did you hear me? I will say it again. When you sleep or are intimate with your wife, you will give secrets. I believe every woman wants to know the secret before you give it to her. Let us be honest. With the exception of blood, your semen is the only thing that comes out of you that has life within it. Everything else that comes out of you is dead, but when it comes to semen, there is life. You have to be very honest with your wife, because your semen is alive. This may be deep for some of you, but I am trying to help men understand that when you have coitus with your wife, you are sharing life. It is time to tell the truth and stop living a lie. It is time to tell true and not lying about life. You heard the phase, but hear it again: the truth will set you free. When you express the truth, you are no longer under the cloud. I'd rather have a cloud of truth versus a cloud of lies. Within the cloud of lies, you do not know the weather patterns, but when you have the cloud of truth, all is well within your mind, body, and soul.

As men, we are used to hiding like our antiquity grandfather (Adam), but it is time to break the curse and make our course in life. In reality, many men carry on the attitudes and cares of their ancestors, but there comes a time when you must destroy the curse. My brother, tell her the truth and nothing but.

Chapter 4:
Tell Before Told

Tell or told are various forms of the same meaning with the difference relating to time. In my opinion, it's more powerful to tell than being found out. To speak the truth, you must find yourself and then tell your wife what you have discovered.

Without a shadow of a doubt, telling on yourself is always better than someone telling on you. I have heard men say that their greatest accountability partner should be their friend. I disagree. Your greatest accountability partner, if you are married, should be your wife. Your wife is your greatest accountability partner because she is one with you. Your friend, family, and associates are not close to you as it relates to your wife. She is your rib, sir, and no other. Due to this, you should tell her first.

A wife would rather hear it from you than from another person. I know there is shame and guilt that a man carries when he sees the sin within his life, but somehow he must battle that sin even if he has not defeated it and tell the truth. You are ahead, because by confessing you are not hiding your stuff from your wife. In reality, you have become naked before her. This is the why God created male and female naked.

In marriage, a wife wants to know specifics, not generalities. This is why she asks many questions. She asks questions to not be in the dark. When you tell your wife, you have headed off a problem before it grows.

In a recent poll by *Men's Health* magazine, the top quality that a woman looks for is not sex, looks, or build, it's honesty. Why? Because trust is a key to a marriage. If she cannot trust you, you cannot build. If you cannot build, you will not grow. If you do not grow, you will eventually die.

All should avoid the sin of dishonesty. Sin is sin, and God will judge for the deeds done in our body. Yet when a man tells his wife all things and she decides to stay with him, at least he is not guilty of the sin of dishonesty.

It is kind of like the theory of before I buy the dog, I'd like to know if it bites and then I know how to deal with it, and the protections I need in dealing with this animal. The same is said toward you, my brother. By telling your wife how you are inside and outside, at least you give her options instead of a guessing game. If you have a STD and do not tell her before you are married, then you are dishonest. However, if you are forthright and say honestly the good, bad, and ugly, then you are a good man, a man who can be trusted.

Women can deal with pain. When a woman has a baby, she knows of the accepted pain that is coming her way. When a woman becomes pregnant, she has an idea of the pain coming her way. The same can be said with your sins. If you tell your wife what you really are before the relationship starts, she then can tell you whether she can or cannot deal with the pain. If she can't deal with the pain, then at least you told her straight up versus her finding out on the birthing table. The birthing table is the start of the relationship. It is the beginning of a union of holy wedlock. By coming clean, you become an honest man to God and her.

Chapter 5:
Make Up Your Mind

If you are confused about your sexuality, you need to stop what you are doing until you discover who you are. Again, scripture is simple when it comes to homosexuality, to which I agree. Yet, I am trying to reach both Christian and non-Christian men to hold their marriages in honor and dignity by being truthful. If you are confused, why keep messing with a woman who has taken on your last name and become your wife? The madness must stop.

I know preachers may say, "Why don't you slam them for their gay activities?" I believe the church has done that to the point of saturation.

Jesus said He came to save the lost and not condemn. In essence, I have no heaven and hell to put anybody in. People know the truth, and yes, the truth will set you free.

Well, the same is said toward a gay man who wants to hit from both sides. You cannot do it and be an Up High or true man. A true man will have his mind up. Can you imagine a general who is not sure of his battle plans? Personally, I would rather be on the enemy's side that has a commanding general.

Men, you are a commanding general of your body and family. If you are back and forth between women and men sexually, then the next best thing to do is stop your actions. We know life is short, and we all need to live in the truth of something. If you do not know what you are supposed to do, why get another person involved within your life when you are not sure of your life yourself? It is unfair to you and your loved ones. I pray, of course, you take the heterosexual way, but if you decide to be gay, then be true to your wife. Tell her the truth about your orientation. Tell her the truth about your sexual proclivities. Just tell her the truth.

And, from the truth, she can decide to walk or stay. On a side note, I hope women who have discovered that their men are bisexual would leave. Why, because this is still adultery. If he were cheating with another woman, a wife would not hesitate to divorce. If that is the case toward the opposite sex, how much more for the same sex. Again, this book will hopefully help men stop the process before things begin.

Hear me, please. I am not encouraging homosexuality. In reality, I am encouraging living in truth. I again agree that homosexuality is a sin. I also agree lying is the simplest and deadliest form of sin as well. What I am saying on the rooftop is that, men, be real to your wives. Let go of your secret.

Hide nothing from her and tell her everything. The more you hide your secret, the less you can hold on to her. Men who are wrestling with their sexuality, I pray for you, because most who wrestle have been abused. It does not make any sense to me to be in torment and bring in another person. This is a selfish act. Therefore, brother, if you are fighting, do not allow your wife in the ring with you.

I do not know any boxer who would permit his wife "in the ring" while fighting. A good man wants his wife to see him box the opponent. In a marriage, this is telling your wife your sexual proclivities. Let her see the pain and sweat that you endure. Do not permit her to guess about the issue. Let her see you fight the issue on a daily basis. Fight the good fight of faith, men, in front of your wives and not behind your wives. She probably knows anyway.

Live in truth and not in lies. Lies will catch up and bite when you least expect it. The Bible says that a double-minded man is unstable. I do not think any man wants a woman who is unstable. One day she is home, and the next day she is not. Such actions are crazy to any man.

If this is crazy for you, the same is crazy for your wife. A wife wants a man whose mind is made up not only in not having another woman, but the same in reference to having only one sexual collaborator.

A wife and sexual partner should be the same person, but because of the day and time in which we live, one cannot assume. A wife cannot assume her husband's sexual energy, so out of respect he must tell on himself and be truthful with his words.

Chapter 6:
Convicted and
Not Condemned

There is a big difference between being convicted and not condemned. In essence, this book will hopefully convict men to tell the God's truth to their spouse. Without such, a man will stay condemned. In all, God is the final judge and one of the judgments He will pass out will depend on how one treated his fellow man.

Your fellow man also includes your spouse. If you treat your fellow man wrong, such will come back. The same is said for men as they relate to their wives. Even the scriptures say to deal with your wife correctly, because such things will hinder your prayer with God (I Peter 3). It is undoubted that the Bible says that when you become married, you become one flesh. Having sex with another represents the unity of one. The only unity of sex that God recognizes is between two committed heterosexuals.

It will take a true man not to stay under the banner of condemned but to move over into the area of convicted. A convicted man will do right whether his wife sees it or not. He can be condemned and still lie, cheat, and steal. However, a convicted man has a conscience.

I pray the men who are reading this book have a conscience. Without a conscience, you will go toward another, have sex with him or her, and bring home potential diseases to one who really loves you.

I pray brothers who read this book have not forgotten the word *conscience*. Many men on the down low have "do not care" attitudes toward their loved ones, but such is not the will of God.

Again, I am expanding the definition of down low to include men who at any time hide from their wives the true essence of themselves. In other words, you are doing activities that you feel are below her radar and doing it is down low. Down low, if you look at it, are two adjectives that almost mean the same thing. To stop "down low" activity, you have to be convicted. Convicted not to lie to your wife or cheat. Whether it is another man or woman, you must remember, my brother, that you made a vow that must not be forsaken.

And you must be convicted, because without it you will take every pair of loins that comes your way and return hurt to the one you truly love. Conviction says no when the flesh says yes. I cannot say you will never be tempted by forbidden fruit, but when it comes, you have to say no. Without saying no, you open yourself to emotional pain that may take a lifetime to deal with.

And men who are straight, like myself, must not in turn quickly put down those who wrestle with homosexuality or down low activity, because, but for the grace of God, there go I. Other men, for whatever reasons, find themselves in this tangled web, but you, dear sirs, have been spared.

Chapter 7:
Legacy You Are Carrying

The practice of blessing the next generation was something done in antiquity. Yet, this is not the case anymore. Some fathers are concerned about getting strange booty more than blessing their sons. Maybe the reason why generations have stayed the same or remained cursed is that fathers have not blessed their children.

I have always been a critic of those who have left more in the ground upon death than on top of the ground. What I mean is that the casket is more expensive in relation to the funds left for the family. In my humble opinion, this is a sin. We have to start blessing our children and creating a legacy that will last a lifetime. In reality, if you are not blessing, you are cursing your children.

I propose that if you do not put a blessing on them, you are really putting a curse on them as well. If a newborn child is placed into an open field without a covering of father or mother (blessing), then that child is doomed to the elements and animals of the area. The same is said for a father who will not bless his child through words and action. Action is especially seen in how the father treats his mother as it concerns truth.

In essence, my brothers, I am saying if you cannot be truthful to your wives, at least do it for your children. Leave a legacy behind that does not only include money and things, but a legacy that "I told the truth to my wife/your mother". From that, your children will pick up the policy of telling the truth.

Many fathers want to leave money and wealth behind, which is fine, but there is nothing like leaving behind truth. I once heard that Jack Nicholson was born out of wedlock, and for almost 30 years, he did not know that his "sister" was really his mother. It almost killed him emotionally, because somebody did not tell him the truth.

Telling the truth is a missed attribute that is lacking in our society today. In reality, people spend money quicker and easier in comparison to the truth. The power of truth will, in reality, keep your heart and mind clean. When you are constantly lying about your life to your wife, you are in reality living a lie. Lies die, but truth remains for eternity. We, as men, must keep the truth before us. We must say, as men, "I'd rather be in truth than a lie." In essence, this process must be kept before your face continually.

You must speak truth. If you do not practice truth, you will practice lies. I say practice because it is so easy to lie and so hard to speak truth. Truth is life while lies are death. But to survive, you must keep truth at its premium. You must say, "I rather have truth than lie."

Many preachers stress holiness. Do not get me wrong. I believe in holiness, too, but truth must be the foundation of holiness. The reason why is because when you lie to yourself, the holiness will not mean a hill of beans. Yet, when you say, "I want truth," you now are about to get blessed in many ways. If God does not get me my heart's desire, I know that I have truth. Truth is more valuable and powerful than money and riches of life.

Back to Nicholson. What a tragedy it would

have been for this man to lose everything because the people whom he knew the most did not speak the truth. In fact, the entire neighborhood knew of Jack Nicholson's origin, yet no one spoke a word. God help us as men to speak the truth to our wives and children. Just as genetic problems are passed along to the children through their fathers or mothers, there are other emotional things passed on that are just as dangerous.

Men who are living on the down low, or other secret issues, must speak the truth. Speak the truth for the sake of your legacy. There are things within our control, men, and one of them is telling the truth. There is no degree or master program that can help you deal with this. We are all full of sin. And, by the grace, we live, move, and have our being, yet without truth, the legacy you pass down will fail and be of no avail.

Lies will not stand the test of time; it is already enough that you live in agony and pain. What type of father are you if you pass down this trait to your children? There is nothing worse than passing down a sin to the next generation without consideration of alerting the kids.

The point of things is to understand that when you accept the truth about yourself and not act self-righteous, you help your children deal with any sin that may be in your life. If you cannot stop an issue, my brother, then you must speak the issue truthfully. Without the truth, you are going to be held down to a point of non-healing. You may have the curse, but at least stop the curse from flowing to the next generation, and this is done by telling the truth all the time. It's hard, but one should want to take and embrace this task.

Chapter 8:
Badge of Shame,
Not Honor

There were many reasons for writing this book, but the main reason was the "supposed" glee down low men had about their dual identity. In my opinion, to have this type of secret from your wife is not a badge of honor, but of shame. Shame because you inflict your wife not only with the physical but emotional pain of carrying on a lie for many years. In addition, when her friends discover your identity, what shame comes on her?

In the superhero plot, one is always trying to get the identity of the hero, hence why they wear the mask. Well, great men are superheroes to their families, but when they come home, they take off the mask to be who they really are.

Yet, this is not the same for men who are down low. Their mask is one of wrong, and they never take it off. A true man knows that his home is a place of rest and not a place to show off his superhuman powers.

You must become transparent to the ones you love. It is a proven fact that women live longer than men. My hypothesis says this is due to stress. Men carry more stress while women, at times, relieve the stress. One stressful point, my brother, is hiding secrets. When you hide or mask a secret, it's stress that keeps it on.

By unmasking yourself, the stress will become less. Why? Because you are not wearing the mask. Nevertheless, the same goes for men who are down low. Take off the mask, brothers, who are on the down low. Those who are hiding other secrets from the ones you love, I say the exact same thing as well. Take off the mask.

In the Disney movie "The Incredibles," all the family members knew their individual powers, strengths, and weaknesses. To be the superhero, you have to be naked before your wife. Any untruthfulness shows the depth of deceit that you ride with on a day-in and day-out basis. Such deceit will eat at your inner core. Another word for down low is hypocrite.

Any Bible scholar will tell you that Jesus' enemies in the world, besides Satan, were the hypocrites. In Matthews 23, He detested such people. Well, much in that case has not changed. God still hates the falseness of those who say one thing but in reality are something different.

Men on the down low are hiding sexual secrets: doesn't your wife deserve better than what she is given? May I say you would not want her to keep secrets from you, so why do it to her? Come out with it and say it.

Be a man about it and not one who hides behind excuses and other points of view. She deserves the truth and not a lie. Again, the Bible condemns homosexuality, with which I agree, but this is not the intention of this book. My intentions are to get men to come out with the truth.

Take the mask off at home, my brother. There is something about exposing yourself before your wife. Not only is it sexual when you see your wife, it is also sexual for her to see you naked. You may have marks and ugliness on your body, but she still wants to see. If there is excitement with being naked before one another, then there is excitement about exposing all things to your wife.

Do not hide or suppress anymore. For men not dealing with down low but with pains of the past, your wife still wants to know. In essence, when you speak, you will heal. Who is to say that whatever issue you deal with may be healed by the confession of the soul? Talk about it and speak the truth in love with power and compassion.

Again, be a man of honor and not of shame. If you should die today, your wife knows she had a man who told her the truth. How ugly it would be that during your funeral a partner tells her the truth. Not only her, but your entire family will suffer.

Since down low brothers do not know what a partner will do, then it is best to tell on yourself. Such a confession about yourself and inner demons deserves medals of honor and praise.

Why a medal? Well, because you had to win some internal battles. You had to fight yourself on a daily basis to see the other side of the rainbow. Such a fight is worth one getting a Medal of Honor and glory.

Men who fight themselves are always worthy of a medal in order to tell the world they made it. They fought the largest and most powerful demon called self. You have to get that Medal of Honor, my brother. The greatest medal you will get is from your wife and children.

Men will give you medals, but it is nothing in comparison to when your own flesh and blood give you one for making their lives better. Yet without the medal, you have nothing to hold up your head. You have to look at your chest to see if you have received the medal yet. If the answer is no, then, brother, the time is now to get your medal.

Without the medal, you have no manhood. In reality, this is why we have more fake than real men. Real men have badges given by their families. I pray and encourage men to see their wives and hold their honor to the best of their ability.

Chapter 9:
Fathers Sexually Abusing
Their Sons

Even though this is not widespread, in my spirit, I believe men are abusing their sons around the world.

As perverted heterosexual men sexually abuse their daughters, I have to believe there are perverted homosexual men who are sexually abusing their sons. No matter how you look at it, this is disgusting.

I am not categorizing all bisexual, homosexual, or down low husbands as abusing their sons, yet we have to go there, which is why the cry throughout this book is to tell the truth.

As messed up as this sounds, we have to know that as little girls are abused on a daily basis, so are little boys. Because we live in a society that is male-based, such abuse by father to son may not be reported due to the manner of the crime and shame. However, let us not be ignorant of the fact that such practices are being performed in America every day. Only God knows what will make men and boy crimes stop, as well as men and girl crimes.

Ladies, may I say that a man is known by his penis. This means as losing a breast is messed up to a woman, so is losing a penis to a man. It is what defines us as men. In addition, one emotional way of losing a penis is being raped by another man. We see the many men who have been fighting emotional abuse because of abuse by a priest, preacher, or prophet, and so it is said for a father who takes such ungodly activities toward his son.

For a son who has abused by the same sex, such pain may be irreconcilable without the power of God and truth. And who is to say that the husband who abuses his child was abused himself by a father or male figure? Society and wives must come to grips with this. Men involved in these activities cannot say that they are very happy with their lifestyles. To not deal with this issue and pass it down to another generation is wrong.

Once again, moms, be careful. Single moms, be especially careful. You may have the next president, doctor, Nobel Peace Prize winner, or great American within your mist. Things are so bad today that you really can't trust anyone but God and yourself.

Again, I ask the down low man to be truthful. God will judge, but when you cause another generation to sin, such will be paid out accordingly. Eli's sons in 1 Samuel 2:12-23 not only sinned, but they made Israel to sin as well. What a powerful statement it is that Eli's sons were the ones who started the issue of men not following God in Israel. They were the ones who in fewer than three generations divided Israel.

In words of compassion, brother, whom will you divide due to your sin? It's one thing to cause your sin, but to cause others to sin? The blood may be on your hands. We all wrestle with sin of some sort. Of that I am convinced. But whatever your sin may be, don't make it pass down to the next generation. Pass on your blessings, not your curses.

Nowhere in the Bible do you see fathers cursing their sons, with the exception of Noah and a couple of others. In all, fathers wanted to pass on a blessing and not a curse. Again, men who are fighting with down low activity do not pass down the curse. In other words, if a father abuses his child, he kills the next generation, because who is to say that the child will be down low? He may become homosexual, meaning there is no next generation.

Chapter 10:
Samaritan Man

There is a passage in the Bible about a woman who was very sinful in stealing five husbands, but Jesus kept talking to her because this woman was HONEST. May I say this to a man who is on the down low and hiding sexual taboos from his wife, come into the light and not the dark.

God wants you to be honest with your wife. Let me quickly define that if you are living an openly gay lifestyle, then I am not talking to you. The word of God is clear on the sin of homosexuality.

I am talking to men who are hiding secrets from their wives that should be spoken. And may I even expand the definition that if you are telling your boys about your most intimate points more than your wife, there is a problem.

The point is that as the woman of Samaritan came clean, we need to do the same things as well. Men who are living double lives, can you take the lead from this woman? The Samaritan woman was able to save her entire city. This is the first and only time under Jesus' ministry that an entire city was saved.

Brothers, if you can be honest, the healing of God will, and shall, come upon you as well. Let the healing begin today.

Yes, I hear men say you are not married to the woman I am with. But we have to take our most intimate points to them. Their attitude does not stop us from telling the truth. We are supposed to be men, not boys. Men face the challenge and move on with it. The point is not them understanding; it's you conveying the truth no matter what.

Brothers who live on the down low, your sins of hiding are only hindering and killing you slowly. Stress is a killer of men. And stress can come from men who have secrets from their wives. I believe somebody said that secrets could kill.

Be a Samaritan man, meaning be a man who tells the truth no matter how embarrassing it may be. Many times, we miss opportunities to speak who we really are, but the time has come. Jesus kept talking to this woman because she spoke the truth. Maybe if she had started lying, Jesus would have walked away.

Jesus knows that, but the bottom line was that the sister kept it real with Jesus. Yes, brothers, first be real with God, and then go to your wives and be real with them. Again, when you become real with your wife, she may not embrace you with love, but at least she has one less thing to deal with, and that is a lying man.

After the woman of Samaritan got the revelation, she went and told the men of the city to come meet the man who had told her all. In essence, after she got truth, she had to tell truth. Sounds like a good message, because it says after the Lord reveals things to you, it is time to go and reveal to others. And yes, I am going to say it; it starts first at home. When the home base is covered, everything is covered.

In essence, brother, you've got to want the light versus the dark. If you want to remain secret, remember the issues and cover-ups you've had to do. I believe Jesus came to this woman when she wanted to change. In other words, don't mess with God unless you want to change a pattern in your life. When you are ready to change, God is ready to deliver.

Let me add this important point. Whatever sin you find yourself in; God is able to deliver you. God in Christ is able to set you free. I am not the one who will judge you. It will be God. Plus, the Lord says that the way I judge you is the way God will judge me.

There is forgiveness, dear sir, at the cross, but you must confess to be blessed.

Chapter 11:
Pastor, Prophet, Preacher, Priest

In no way am I making a swiping condemnation spirit on my spiritual profession. Yet, while the Catholic Church was hammered due to the sins of messed-up priests having sex with minors, the Protestant Church was quiet.

The issue is that there are preachers who are lying not only to their congregations but also to their wives. I have no documented statistics at all concerning this problem. All I know is that the down low problem is within some pulpits. Yes, there are men and women in our pulpits who must examine themselves about what persons or children they are messing up. May I add that no preacher is without sin, but to go around and spread your sin to people who depend upon thy word is a problem. This portion is also extended to preachers who say one thing, but do exactly the opposite. In other words, if you are going to preach on a sin that you struggle with, you had better come with grace and not damnation.

We must examine ourselves daily to ensure that we have no secrets from our wives. Secrets, as stated, will kill you. Again, this is why the pulpit must not be hypocrites in any way. I profess that maybe preachers should get up and tell their membership that they are not Jesus Christ, but sinners saved by grace. I know some prophet, apostle, or "titled" preacher is going to disagree, but people want real preachers, not a hypocrite mind-frame.

In other words, what you preach, you live. If you are not living it, then either confess to your wife or tell the congregation to pray for you. I am not sure why we think we are infallible. We are not, and never will be.

Let's not act surprised, because many people, including the pulpit, have blamed many things on the devil, and yes, some have justified raping and taking the flock because of their false order in God. No orders supersede God's divinity order. Those who go to the sacred desk cannot have any type of sex with the flock. This is an abomination. And by having sex with the flock, you will be judged by God. Having sex with a flock member, in my opinion, is spiritual incest. I know many will disagree and justify their sin toward a member. Yet, this is wrong no matter how you flip it. Just like a child molester is on the bottom pole in the jail, so do I feel pastors who "rape" their flocks are on the bottom pole with God. Because after that preacher zips up his pants or puts on her skirt, that person is messed up for eternity.

Preachers who are doing this, go home, repent, and confess to your wives. You may need to get another job occupation. For those who are abused, go to the authorities and speak the truth. And yes, I understand that the "adult" abused has some responsibility for the abuse, but in reality, the pastor or preacher is in "control" of the situation because of his authority role.

This is why I believe a preacher's greatest accountability partner should be his wife, and not another brother at another church. For all the wife knows, that best friend could be the "other man." How messed up that is, but we've got to go there. I would tell all first ladies to investigate their husbands if they spend more time with their preacher friends than with their wives. If their husbands are always going on trips and to conferences together, those wives must investigate.

If a pastor is always going on trips with the same guy, or guys, for weeks on end and never coming home, and has not given his wife some good loving in at least two days, something is wrong.

I say again, if a brother is not with his wife intimately after a week back from his "seminar," something is wrong. Yet, in the morning you see his loins still working, something is wrong. When I mean working, I mean erections. So, if the erection is working, and he is not having a relationship with his wife for more than a week, there must be a problem somewhere in his body.

What I am doing is just trying to get brothers to tell the truth. Is there a convention every week, brother, that you have to stay in the "same room" with another preacher? I do not care who it is, if a pastor is always going on a convention in the same room with another preacher, something is wrong. I know I am going to get some letters on this, but again, I am just giving my opinion.

In the church, some men were raised by mothers or autocratic fathers, and thus some are not sure of their own sexual orientation but they still have the title of preacher. Let me say, you can be anointed and still in sin. Yes, ask David and Samson. Many men are anointed, but it does not mean they are not being truthful about themselves.

The key is not that sin will be in you; the key is will you lie or condemn others about the same issue you wrestle with. This is the key of every Christian. Yes, God can take a faulty bottle, but he can't take a bottle that will not admit it is faulty.

On another note by revelation, sometimes these gospel concerts are pick-up times for men on the down low who are looking for other guys who share their lust. With this statement, I am only trying to expose problems that exist within our churches. Can you believe that men are going to conventions to just find another man on the down low? Going to conventions just to find sex is a sin and abomination. The devil is a liar. In reality, preacher, all you need is at your house.

Making conventions into a place of prostitution is wrong. There will be hell to pay to those concert and convention organizations that purposely take care of these types of issues. This book may not be popular, but this book will be the truth.

Chapter 12:
Gay Porn

Porn is wrong. Yet there are men who struggle with this. Most men have been affected by some lust problem whether in picture or real time. I can only direct them to the cross.

Also, a man cannot condemn one without condemning himself. Pride and strippers are just as wrong as porn. Abusing your wife emotionally is just as wrong as watching porn. Being a controlling husband is just as wrong as a sex chat room. A flirting and manipulating husband is just as wrong as Internet porn. Sin is sin.

But without a doubt, a heterosexual man, can't watch, or even stand, gay porn. This doesn't make him a bigot. This is only fact. Watching two men corn hole each other is not a turn-on for any true heterosexual man. And do not give me "I am only interested by the thought of two men getting it on." That is bull. Husbands, hear me: if you are watching men go at each other sexually, you are down low.

Yet, if you watch such, you are on the down low. Even though you may have not done the act, you've seen it committed. Yes, porn is an issue, and again I am not trying to condemn, but if a man is watching gay porn, he is on the down low.

The issue of porn has been within society for a long time, yet one thing is sure. If a man is watching and enjoying gay porn, he is down low. Ladies, do not let him fool you that he is just curious. There is not enough curiosity in the world that will make a man want to watch gay porn unless he is gay.

Again, we are after the truth of why you are doing one thing and saying something different. Wives, if you have found gay porn in your husband's closets, don't let him wiggle out of it. He is either gay or thinking about doing gay things. No doubt.

Wives, let me tell you that we men are visual

creatures, and we love to look. If a man is honest with you, he will tell you that he enjoys sex on a regular basis. Men, as a whole, sleep, eat, and think about sex on a daily basis. Well, in that case, if he has porn and ANY percentage of it is gay, then he is on the down low. There is no lie detector needed; he is gay.

Let us not fool each other. There is an epidemic of bleeding hearts that have been killed by men who have not been honest.

Do not deny the truth. If a man watches it, he wants to participate. Some ladies may ask, why porn? Because for husbands, it is an easy way to have sex without going through the emotions of wining and dining his wife. Major issues with porn include deceit, lying, and men forsaking their wives totally for their fantasy. I am not saying fantasies are wrong, but when you live in your fantasies more than real life, something is wrong.

It seems like the bisexual agenda is cute in movies and such, but a down low man is not cute or humorous. It is dishonorable. Why? Because you become the Trojan horse, from Greek mythology, to your own house. You let strangers into your own house that in so many ways could destroy everything you've worked hard for. Again, looking at gay porn, in my humble opinion, does make you down low, especially if you are married to a woman.

A woman deserves better than a lie. When you are married and keep secrets from your wife, in the end destruction will come.

Again, I go into this subject for wives who deal with the sin of porn with their husbands. Yet, for her husband to have a gay porn selection, something is terribly wrong. There is no doubt in my mind that he is wrestling with his sexual identity.

Chapter 13:
Women Do It, Too

I'm not sure what you call a woman on the down low, but it happens as well. I can't leave out men who have been betrayed by wives who went out with another woman in a sexual manner.

As I have spoken to men, I speak to women to do the same in reference to telling the truth. Hear your heart and be truthful to it. I know many may say, "Pastor, are you giving a license to sin?" The answer is no. What I am saying is that our country is full of men and women who lie to themselves on a daily basis. Such hypocrites will only keep you away from

God and from each other.

Why? The Gospel of John says we worship God in Spirit and truth. If you lie to yourself and those around you, then you are not in contact with God. So, ladies, as I have spoken to the men, I speak to you to be truthful and erase that guilt of cover-up. How can God save you when you are still in denial or lies?

May I say that some Christians are saved liars? In other words, they are confessing salvation but are covering up their true selves. This is wrong and incorrect. As we have mostly spoken to men that this is wrong, I speak to women the same way. You can't go in God with lies.

I think we will never see a "reality" Christian family on TBN or the Word Network because we are not ready to speak truth and life that we are not perfect.

As goes for men, the same must be said for women who are down low. No excuse, my sisters. Falling in love with the same sex is wrong according to God's word, but even more important is for your husband not to know what you are doing is wrong. Two wrongs don't make a right. You can't justify creeping around on your husband. Such things are not allowed or praised by God.

I encourage all sisters to confess if they are doing it. I know it may be a dream of a man to have two women making out, but such is adultery. Yes, even when both parties agree. I believe the bed is big enough for only two married heterosexual people and two people, no more.

This subject may be too heavy for the mother and missionary board, but there are lesbians even in the house of God, who are looking to take silly women to points of darkness never seen before. And, yes, I hear those who say that they tried to fall in love with a man and were raped emotionally and physically repeatedly. This may be true, but the means does not justify the wrong that one has.

My sister, your heart may be hurting, but you still can't go over onto the side of that. To be loved is a beautiful thing, but just doing it for physical and emotional pleasure is not enough. Even if strong women in your church or family are pressing you, the condition is still the same, that homosexuality and adultery are wrong.

Again, this book is not to convict, but to help brothers and, yes, sisters, to be honest with their loved ones. Being honest is pleasing in God's eyesight. Yes, I have heard women say that because of the pain caused by a man, they have become involved in a same-sex relationship. I know the pain may be real. When you are attached, you job is not to stay in the pain. In reality, your object of power is healing from the pain. When you don't heal from it, it will attack you in many ways. Being raped emotionally by the unfaithfulness of a man in your life does not give you a license to tip out on your man.

When a woman becomes sexual with another woman because of the pain caused by the man, the will of God is not in her. Some have by God's grace turned this situation around. Don't become bitter but better. You must press beyond the point of pain. Your husband's treatment of you is not the stopping point for you.

Chapter 14:
Women Have
Suffered Enough

Women have suffered enough because of the crap with men from their past. Men on the down low, is this what you want your wives to remember you by? Adding unnecessary pain in your wife's life because of the dishonesty that you had is not the will of God in any way. A woman deserves more than your lies. She deserves more than your hiding, tripping, and skipping points of view. If you are not careful, whatever you reap, you will also sow within your life.

You giving your wife additional pain after she

births your baby and such, and then you turn around and say you love her. Yet how can you say you love her after having sex with your down low partner? This is not love in any shape or fashion. In reality, it is bad karma.

This will kick back to you in the end. There is no way such behavior would be accepted by you, my brother. If this is the case, why do it? A woman expects a man to stand up for her and not put her down, and give her the proper respect.

The ultimate proper respect for a woman is a man who will keep his penis home. The car is nice and the money is fine, but ultimately, what she wants to know is that her man is faithful to her. Not only faithful from another woman, but more so, faithful from another man.

Due to our culture of stealth activity, more men are creeping with men instead of creeping with their wives. In other words, your wife is able to be as freaky as you want to be as long as she knows you are faithful to her. Read my book *New Sheets* to get more info on this.

Men, it's time to stop the pain. We will give some pain to our wives. Actually, there are times we will hurt them more than love them in certain situations. But one situation that should not ever be discovered is that you were unfaithful, especially with another man. In contrast, if you are about to marry and are gay, the most honorable thing to do would be to tell the truth, the whole truth, and nothing but the truth. From there, let your bride make her decisions.

I tell brothers everywhere to reveal the truth about all things in their lives. Stop lying and be truthful with the one you love.

When you reveal who you are in the beginning, she can, in turn, make the decision to stay or leave you. The one thing that a woman wants more than anything is a truthful man.

Yes, we are making more money than ever in our lifetimes, but this is not enough. The rings, things, and bling are good, but she wants you. She wants you. This is a hard fact for men to understand. Furthermore, when you give her yourself, don't be shocked and surprised that she doesn't believe that you are telling the truth.

Many men have come to me and said, "Pastor, I am telling the truth NOW, but she does not believe me." Well, when you plant bad seed, it may take a while for the bad harvest to go away. I know you want to go forward in your life, but she can't. This kills and stops men from being truthful, but if you can wade through the pain, there is a blessing on the other end. Don't give up, because she did not give up on you. If she didn't give up on your way, don't give up on her at this particular point in your life.

If your wife has pain, let it at least be expected pain. In other words, let her know before it's coming what you are doing. In childbearing, the woman is always given a warning before the labor pains get stronger. The same principle should work for us as men. We know when we are about to do something in error. Just add the caveat of telling the truth. This will in some way lower the shock value.

If anything, women are being shocked about the true sexual nature of their men all over this country. Yes, ladies who are reading this book, understand that men are freaky. The key to a man is to tell the extent of his freaky side. This should be done before the ceremony, because in doing this, the man supplies the matrimony shock absorbers before things really hit his wife. Again, brothers, tell the truth, even if it means you lose everything. You would rather lose everything and keep your integrity as it relates to your wife. Please, brothers, speak the truth.

Chapter 15:
Women's Decisions

This chapter is dedicated and encourages women to not take just any man. Let me warn you, no man is perfect. Yet a woman should not have to fight for her husband's attention from another woman, and certainly not from another man.

When a man goes with another man while married or engaged to another woman, he, in words, is saying that he prefers males to females, and a woman should not have to share her man with anybody.

So in essence, women, do a thorough

investigation of your man. Find out who he really is. Yes, even test him to see if he will tell a lie or not. If he lies about one thing, he may lie about his sexual orientation.

Again, this book is not about saying homosexuality is a sin. I believe the gay community knows that. In essence, this book is written to tell men to be honest with their spouses and for women to deal with the truth.

Ladies, you MUST demand truth from your men. If you have misgivings, check them out before you go further into the relationship. It is much easier and less messy to leave a relationship within the dating stage versus the married stage.

Don't run into a marriage. Marriage is a lifetime commitment, so should you not make a lifetime investigation of a man who is going to be within your life forever?

Yes, check out his orientation. Yes, check out his orientation. A heterosexual will always be attracted to the opposite sex and repulsed by same sex coitus action. Just the idea of seeing two men go at it will make him go crazy. This, again, does not change.

A man will not just switch from loving women to men in one day. It was there all the time. I understand others have abused men when they were children. Ladies, you have to ask him about his childhood. And, ladies, don't be dumb. God has given you a lie detector inside you. Trust your senses.

Men may read this book and say I am coming down hard on them. I have to, because races and generations depend on us. Women have carried the burden for too long. It's time for us to step up. We have to tell the truth. It starts with our loins.

Yet, even if a man is wrestling with sexuality, he needs to be honest with you. You may ask, "How do I know if my man is down low or real?" It's called prayer, time, and talking to his friends. If you take him to a mall or movie with beautiful girls and his member never moves, or if you talk to him in a suggestive way and nothing happens, then something is wrong. Check out his male friends. This, I believe, is the biggest telltale sign to see if a man is on the down low or not.

If he wants to go to a private place every week and will not report to you his whereabouts, you may have a man who is hiding a secret. Even when it comes to sexual sessions, a real man will not go for transgender or bisexual sex. There is nothing more beautiful than the female body. A woman is something beautiful in all shapes and sizes.

Therefore, for a man to say he all of a sudden wants the same sex, it was there all the time. Hear me, sisters. That is why you've got to take your time and inspect the man. I know you are lonely and all, but you have to inspect this man. Just getting a man is not the point. The point is to have a man who will be honest and love you all the way.

Do not take half a man as a husband. And please don't think that you can change him. You can't and will not do it. Changing a man's sexuality will not be done by having sex with him. You can't change a man by marrying him. In fact, this will only make him want to stay in his secret more. I have heard women say that they can change him, but in reality, the man has changed her by lowering her standards considerably.

Renting a man from somewhere else is not the will of God in any shape. God does not give partial blessings. If God does not give partial blessings, why have a partial man? God does not want the plan in your life. God wants a man in your life who will take care of you and be whatever he says to you in essence.

I know the pool of good men is small, but don't give up, ladies. Do not lower your standards just because you want to tell everyone that you are married. Let me say quickly that no man is perfect. Every man will have a problem in his life; the key is to get the man to tell you want it is. If a man will not confess the pain, then he is not the man for you in any way, shape, or fashion in your life. Just wait for God to bring the right man to you.

The sexuality of a man really tells who he is and isn't. You can't change a man's colors like that overnight. Such things will not be done. Ladies, do not take the bait.

I must say it again. What makes his loins grow? If it isn't you or another female, then you've got a brother on the down low. This, of course, does not include ED. Case in point, when he kisses you, does he grow? If he does not enlarge on a consistent basis, then you might want to check things out.

If, after marriage, he never wants to be intimate and especially on the wedding night, he does not want to have sex, then you might need to get an annulment. If a man never starts sex, ladies, you must ask questions. He may not be on the down low, but he may have some pains of the past. After continual asking and things are still not moving, you might want to be concerned, very concerned.

A woman does not like being in the dark, so again I implore every man who is living a damnable double life to come out of the darkness. A wife deserves a truthful man.

Chapter 16:
If You've Got an Up-high Brother, Ladies, LOVE HIM to DEATH OR WEAR HIM OUT, WHICHEVER COMES FIRST

Simply put, ladies, if you have a man who is not down low, love him to death and wear him out sexually. Do this because of the celebration that you have a man who has come clean with you.

Some wives have destroyed the emotional point of a sensitive brother who is not down low. And while they did this, they drove him to another woman. Yes, ladies, he should have been strong enough to resist the temptation, but he did not, so in part, you are a victim of your own crime.

Sex is God-made. It seems that God gave man a heavy deposit of it. Thus, a man has the unction for the function. In saying that, men who have been clean and honest with their wives should reap the harvest. As a wife reaps the harvest of the diamond rings, clothes, and other tangible things, so should a man receive, without question, the prize of cohabitation with his wife.

Some may ask, "What if he is a freak?" Well, the answer is simple. Do you want him to be a freak with you or somebody else? "Freak" in this point means wanting sex a lot. When it comes to the variety of sexual positions this can only be done by healthy communication between husband and wife.

Some of you ladies must be honest and say that when your husband came to you with a sexual request or fantasy, you freaked out. Once again, would you rather he went to somebody else? The answer is no. I am not saying you have to do everything he says, but you do have to listen with an ear or think about it. And if you think about it and come up with a decision not to do it, then have a good alternative.

Women love to shop. Many would shop until they drop. Well, ladies, men are no different when it comes to sex. Just as a wife would shop until she drops, a husband would have sex until he drops, too.

There are things done by women that men will never understand. No Oprah, Dr. Phil, and such will give us an answer to that. Well, ladies, there are some sexual taboos that your man may have and instead of talking about the evil, understand his healthy desire to have sex. You may not understand his impulse to have sex, but you have to hear and come up with the compromise. If your man will talk, will you listen? Don't you want your husband to listen and talk with you? The same is said when having sex.

Give his sexual fantasies to him every now and then, and ask him to do the same for you. No, he can't force these things on you, but in return, you've got to help him deal with his lust. These are real issues, even in the church. Your man has an appetitive for sex. If he comes to you with these passions and you knock him out, why would he want to come back to you again?

Ladies, men look. And again, gentlemen, when the wife catches you looking, be honest and say yes. Ladies, again, male sexuality will make him do things that will blow your mind, but in essence, through talk and understanding, you will comprehend the drive instead of cursing the drive. As long as he is driving you, isn't this the important aspect? Wake up, ladies, your man has needs, and you are the answer.

No lady would want to have someone mess up her hair after having it done because it is a sensitive point. Well, men are varied the same when it comes to sex. Don't laugh, but take it seriously, because to a man, his sex organ is serious business.

The above can only be done if the brother is honest and not on the down low. If a man wants to be treated like a king, he must respect the queen.

When the man comes to you with a fantasy, your answer is not to say, "Go find a prostitute," As Destiny's Child says, "You better cater to him." The song is powerful and true. Any man doing right wants a woman taking care of his needs from beginning to end. We want a woman to say, "You are good to me, so I've got to be good to you." With that mind frame, you are preparing for a great blessing in your life.

Chapter 17:
Mom Must Expose

This section might be tough, but true. I believe if anyone knows that a person is down low it would be the mother. Without a doubt, a mother knows her son even more than a father at times.

And a mother can't say that a good dose of marriage can heal the down low blues. No, I say the only way is truth. And it starts with Mom being forthright with both her son and future daughter-in-law.

A mother is not a failure if her son grows up gay or down low. It is his decision, not yours. Yet, it is a failure to not tell anyone who desires to marry him the truth. In essence, the mother or father has a responsibility to not condemn but love and comfort a son who may be within this lifestyle.

Most importantly, if he decides to stay in the sin in addition to marrying a female, it is a warning sign that cannot be denied. It's up to the parents to stop any such wedding. To not reveal the truth is a failure to the family.

The scriptures say that they who know to do well and does it not to him, it is a sin. This goes for parents who know what their son is doing. You can't continue to hide things and expect the darkness not to come through. It will not work. I know you do not want to embarrass your son, but what's more important: truth or popularity?

Well, mother-in-law, let's look a little deeper Will you be blessed with yourself if you find out that your first grandchild is HIV positive? I don't think so. I believe that child brought in the world should be given a full chance to survive and not half a chance to survive in the midst of life. In other words, can you look at that child and say with a straight face, "I knew your father, my grandson, was gay, but because of community and pride, I kept this secret? Yet, in a few years your daddy may die, your mother may become widowed or die, and you (grandchild) may die as well."

I don't believe any knowledgeable person would allow such issues to happen. Because you did not open up your mouth, you may see more funerals of youth instead of seniors. Mom or Dad, you must talk to your son. If he stays in the sin of homosexuality, you've got to talk to your future daughter-in-law.

Yes, these are strong, but true, things. A mother and father never stop parenting. Well, when it comes to the bedroom, such things are also profound as well. Mothers, your job can't stop, especially when it comes to your son with another woman.

Mother, if you are not sure, then it is a question that needs to be answered by your son. There could be many reasons why such has occurred. Yet still, it does not make sense to continue the bleeding; it's time for healing to begin for you and your son if he is on the down low.

He or she who knows to do well and does it not to him, it is sin. 1 Sam (3:13): "For I have told him that I will judge his house forever for the iniquity which he know; because his sons made themselves vile, and he restrained them not." This scripture rings true. If you know and do not tell, you will be judged because you failed to keep the truth that was before your eyes.

Chapter 18:
Up High (UH)

Brothers, this book is quite simple. If you act up high (UH), there is no problem that you and your wife cannot handle. Deciding to act UH has benefits.

Overall, your spouse wants an UH man. A UH man is good to his wife and kids. Not perfect, but good and honest. The normal man can be down low, but an UH takes a man of great strength and honesty.

As we all know, even though an animal is called a bird does not mean it is a flying bird. Well, every man has a penis, but that does not mean he has the potential to be an UH man.

UH men are unique and rare. If a woman finds one, she is blessed. If a man turns himself into an UH man, then he finds peace within himself. Men are four times more likely than women to commit suicide. This is due to the internal fight that men have on a day-in/day-out basis. The best cure that I know is becoming an UH man. An UH man does have fears, but he also has bravery to face his fears and shortcomings.

I know a man would not want a wife to never have intercourse with him. Well, the same goes for you, man. If you are doing something in the dark, the wife wants and needs to know about it.

Chapter 19:
Animal Crackers

We are about to hit home base on the subject of men not having secrets, but before we do, let's learn some points of relationships from the animal kingdom.

For those men who are trying to turn the corner on this subject of hiding things, this may be a refresher course for you as you relate to your wife. As you come out of secrets, you will have to learn new skills to ensure the marriage does not go down that path again, the path of having secrets.

I believe, as men, there is a lot we can learn

from the animal kingdom. Although this book is about men telling their wives their secrets, I believe reading about the mating patterns of living animals will hopefully give men ideas for communicating and loving their wives.

Without a doubt, men stay in the dark because of guilt and shame. Such emotions will keep the man in the dark, which will keep his whole family following suit, because how a man goes, so does his family. Enjoy these tips and learn in a light moment. Basic information about the sexual habits of the wild kingdom comes from a book called *"How Animals Have Sex: A Guide to the Reproductive Habits of Creatures Great and Small"* by David Strom. I would suggest buying this book and learning how God set up sex for animals. Though some of the views I will not condone, the book is quite valuable for understanding animals' sexual behavior.

NEMATODE (WORMS)

Many do not know that some nematodes' genitals grow to hundreds of times their original sizes, a point I know some men wish would happen on a daily basis. Yet, many doctors and wives agree that a large penis is not the answer to good sex.

Size does not matter. The average penis size is five to seven inches. It is how you use the organ. Many men are infatuated with the size of the penis and believe a bigger penis will make them great lovers. There is the motivation for pumps and surgery that men undertake to grow their penises.

In reality, a wife would prefer a significant increase in love, patience, and communication than an increase in penis size. In fact, to really make a wife go crazy, she would love an increase in penis size and communication. This combination would take her over the top.

Men, we see the problem, but we have no clue about the solution most of the time. Men, the clue is not a bigger penis but a greater sense of what your wife needs on a day-in/day-out basis.

As Napoleon was a small general who conquered the world, so is a small penis. The clitoris is not deep inside the vagina. The clitoris is near the opening of the vaginal area. And since most women have orgasms by the clitoris and not the vagina, this is the point that men need to focus on.

The clitoris is homologous (mirror image) to the penis. Thus, the penis is more at home to the clitoris than to the vagina. So men, to pleasure your wife, map your penis to the clitoris to ensure your wife's orgasms.

Again, men, the clitoris is a small-elongated

erectile organ at the anterior part of the vulva. In parting, we men need not focus on our desires versus our wives'. If we would take the same energy we have about our size and put our energy toward communication and loving our wives, our marriages would improve significantly.

GIANT PANDA

The female panda has a two- or three-day window in which she can get pregnant within a year. The name of the game for a male panda is timing. Timing is a companion of communication. You can speak to your wife, but if the timing is off, you will not get a great opening in the end.

The male panda has to wait. Husbands, yes there are times we have to wait for the right time and place to make our move. A wife may not hate a quickie, but not ALL THE TIME. A wife wants to know that you think she is worth the time. Many husbands will attest to the time when the wife took a long time to get dressed for something. Yet after you waited, you were blessed with a beautiful creature.

The same is said for a wife who sometimes plays hard to get. But just like a husband cannot do quickies all the time, the wife cannot play hard to get all the time. There must be a spirit of compromise and agreement within the partnership.

BONOBO

The bonobo chimpanzee has many bad points that I don't like. This includes having sex among their family as well as having orgies with every occasion, but there are good points that I must examine.

One of the good points that I love is that when bonobo chimpanzees get into an argument among themselves, instead of fighting, they have sex. I know I am in a dream world, but how many marriages would be different if couples had sex instead of fighting when arguments occurred? Just having sex does not solve problems between the two. Communication is important but having sex after a good discussion would temper the high divorce rate in America.

Another bad point: bonobo chimpanzees have sex with anyone they see. WE, who are in a committed relationship, cannot do such. Our sex is ONLY regulated between husband and wife.

Yet, if couples could adjust on those "anointing moments" instead of fighting or arguing about an issue . . . let's have sex and we promise not to bring it up again. I know, wives, this is a dream for men. If this could happen, we would have more discussions with you, because we would know that it would end up in sex.

We know how to fight and keep bitterness in marriages. Maybe it's time to start to love more. When you love, you marriage is blessed and grows. Please remember that love needs to be the bedrock in a marriage all the time. We need to understand that when we fight and devour one another, what is left?

In all, the bonobo warns us about being oversexed. Sex is good, but within the correct boundaries. Your wife is not a blow-up doll. Your wife is a human being who needs to know that she does not only have a freaky husband, but has a loving husband who wants to know her in many ways.

BARNACLE

We told you earlier that some animals have grown a penis that is longer and bigger than their bodies. Well, the barnacle is just that. Because barnacles are stuck to rocks, they have a penis that is up to thirty feet long. Yes, men, you heard me correctly: thirty feet long. The point is that the barnacle, to me, represents long distance love that reaches out to their mate no matter what.

The barnacle proves that he will go to any length to reach his wife. There are times when men must reach out and touch their wives. We, as men, know how to tap our wives in the night with our penis. But can we take a page from the barnacle and touch our wives' emotions when they are so distant from us for various reasons?

The male penis of the barnacle understands that the female cannot move, so the male penis of the barnacle reaches out. Men, sometimes our wives may be stuck in a certain mind frame or attitude as it relates from topics A to Z, but we must reach out to them. Men, we must reach out to our wives and not just for sex, but because we love them.

Our wives go through a lot. This includes dealing with us and having kids and other pressures in life. Yet, if we, as men, can learn to reach out to our wives, they will be more prone to be open to us, because they see the commitment.

Another point is that the barnacle has to dig deep to reach his mate. Many men give up too quickly in reaching their wives. We have to be like a gold digger who willing to go deep to find the gold.

A husband has to sign up for the commitment and not look back on the hurdles that the wife may put in front of him. And, husbands, be honest; some of the hurdles were caused by you.

RATTLEBOX MOTH

The male rattlebox moth is powerful because when the male has sex, it passes along anti-spider powers. This is needed because when a spider tastes the female rattlebox moth, it repels him. This is all because of good sex with the male rattlebox. By eating rattlebox plants, the male passes the anti-venom to her in his semen.

The major point this brings out is the power to protect and secure the female. A wife wants to have protection. She wants to know that her husband is there to help and not to hurt. She wants to know that her husband is not going to bring back a STD and kill her along the way.

In those bad cases, men can become the major predator to their wives. We, as husbands, should protect and love our wives. Our job is to give them a last name that they can be proud of. Our job is to cover them when they need a helping hand. If we cannot help them, then we hurt them in many ways.

SCORPION

I like to point out that sometimes during sex the male scorpion may sting the female while having sex. This is a point that we should be concerned about. If any couple is reading this, they must take the necessary steps to stop the physical fighting.

It does not mean the fighting will stop, but the physical and emotional hurt is something that is not needed in a marriage. Many times, the fighting comes from what spouses have learned from their parents. If you saw your father fight and hurt, this same trait may be handed down to your family. Couples must take the necessary steps to stop the hurting. We have to change our flag from scorpions to doves.

HONEYBEE

I dare any man to compare his love to the male honeybee. When the male bee is mating with the queen, halfway into the lovemaking his genitals snap off in the queen and he dies. How powerful is that male bee? Can you imagine only making love one time in your life and then dying? If this was in the minds of men, their lovemaking would count and they would do it right, because their first time would be their last time.

Oh, how men would change their lovemaking and treatment of their wives if they had the mind frame of the male honeybee. A male would know that when he loves his woman, he does it to death. What a change of mind this offers for men around the world. Affairs would be extinct and would not be in vogue as they are today.

Today, sex for some husbands is a hobby instead of an honor. An honored woman will give herself to her husband without regard or rejection. Oh, the life of the honeybee is quite strong in my mind, because he gives his life for his queen.

Men all around the world need to say to their wives, "I pledge my life for you. After Christ, you are the most important person within my life, and I must protect you, my queen." Some husbands see their wives as whores or girls. No sir, she is your queen.

When you treat her like a queen, that makes you automatically a king. You cannot have a queen without a king and vice versa. Some men see their wives as witches with a "b," but maybe your wife feels that way because you treat her that way. If you can change your attitude to treating your wife like a queen, all things would change in your household. I believe the way you treat your wife is how she responds back to you. Treat her like a dog, and she will be a bitch to you. If you treat her like a queen, then you will be made a king.

Every man should take a deep look within his soul at how he treats his wife. We must have the male honeybee mind frame and love our wives to death. Do not love her to life; love her to death. This means you pledge everything to her because with Christ, she is everything.

Treat your wives right, men, and they will treat you right. State to your wife your pledge of love, dedication, and honesty. Such points will put her in comfort to know that she has a man who really loves her and is willing to die for her. The word of God says that a husband should love his wife as if Christ loves the church. Did not God give His life for His church? We, as husbands, should do the same.

PAPER NAUTILUS (OCTOPUS)

This male has a detachable penis and dies after it leaves him. A vibrator has nothing on this octopus. It is unbelievable to me, but the male sends his penis toward his woman and dies.

To me, this represents that a husband understands that his penis does not just belong to him but to his wife as well. Husbands, your penis belongs to your wife. Wives, your vagina belong to your husband. Yet, the point is simple that the octopus gives all to his mate.

The male Paper Nautilus will never see the female again, but he gives all to her. Oh, if men would dedicate themselves to their wives, all issues would be taken care of between fighting spouses. This would not be such an issue among men who would surrender all to their wives. In addition, not just in sex, but in life. When a man gives all to his wife, she can trust him. This is very important for a marriage to work.

BEAN WEEVIL

Some husbands and many wives do not like how the penis looks. Yet men, you have nothing on the male bean weevil. His penis is covered with spikes and barbs. How about that? The point that this animal gives us in our human life is being comfortable with the respective penis and vagina. Some husbands and wives seriously struggle in this department because they do not like how their sexual organs look.

There must come a point that the woman becomes comfortable with her labia and the man becomes comfortable with his penis. Despite how "bad looking" their parts are, the weevil still procreates. For us as humans, we need sex not just for procreation but also for relationships.

For Christians, that last statement is a big one. The church has taught in some areas that sex is just for procreation and that's it. No one speaks about orgasms and such. It's not just for procreation. Sex is for both husband and wife to enjoy to the fullest. Yet, to get to this point, married couples must get beyond the look of their sexual apparatus and love.

ATELOPUS FROG

These creatures can be connected sexually for over more than months. Two months of lovemaking is a record in my book. In my mind, this brings up the point of men who are pre-ejaculators.

To this day, many men wonder why their wives do not want to have sex with them. For the most part, it may be for three reasons: 1) she was abused before you married, 2) you have treated her inappropriately, and 3) you ejaculate prematurely.

Husbands should always try to eliminate the easy hurdles within their marriage. Point one takes time, point two takes a little less time, but point three can be fixed NOW with practice.

Premature ejaculators must work on control so that their wives will have more orgasms. A wife who has orgasms has no problems in loving her husband in a sexual way. So, in essence, if you learn how to last, your wife will have no issues being with you sexually.

For men who just cannot get this and no, you do not have to necessarily learn new positions; be a gentleman and let her come first. Before you get yours, husbands, let your wife enjoy first.

Husbands, ask your wife what pleases her and do not be surprised if she says something that is non-sexual. Remember, men, your wife wants to be stimulated emotionally first and then sexually. So, once you deal with the emotions, let her teach you how to please her. I guarantee you will enjoy every lesson.

PORCUPINE

This is no surprise, but the female porcupine is not in the mood a lot. But when she is, it is an amazing thing. It is amazing because although quills cover her entire body, her reproductive organs are not covered with quills. There's a lot humans can learn from this.

The point is that inside every hard-nosed non-sex wife is a soft and sensitive side that every man has to find. Many men are dealing with hard wives, yet I believe before the wife became bitter, she was sweet. The challenge of every man, as for a male porcupine, is to find her open soft side.

While having sex, the male porcupine keeps his hands up to avoid being stabbed. Get the wisdom of this, husbands. Every man wants to get close to his wife, but bitterness and past abuse may have affected her, so while you love, you must be CAREFUL.

I believe every wife desires to love, but due to past or present circumstances, she is unable to set herself free. So, in loving your wife you must be careful, husband, because if not, you will get stabbed in many ways.

The porcupine gives every husband no excuse to not try again. This is especially true when you have caused her to go from sweet to bitter. As discussed in New Sheets, many men have turned their wives like Lot turned his wife.

I know the Lord turned her into a pillar of salt, but if Lot had walked with her instead of in front of her, she might not have turned. Many men are walking in front of their families so far that when their families are in danger, the men are not near to help or protect.

Husbands, no matter how big your goals are, those goals mean nothing if your family is not there to enjoy the blessings of the Lord. Men can be so goal-oriented that they can lose sight of their family. In no way is this the will of God within a husband and wife. We men are goal-oriented, but that should not take the place of God and family.

PRAYING MANTIS

For reasons even too heavy for me, this will be a homework assignment. I will tell you it's very gruesome. If this is any hint, you do not want to marry or have sex with a praying mantis. Another hint is that the male praying mantis never sees his children.

RHINOCEROS

Before you can get with Ms. Rhinoceros, you have to head butt. We are talking about one-ton animals running at each another at full speed. If the male falls down, then he is not worthy of the female. A man must understand that if he marries a strong woman, she will challenge him.

Due to upbringing, some women mistrust men. So, with men, such women are always head butting. A smart man will try to understand why his wife is a certain way. You cannot say that she is a bad person without trying to find why she is that way.

Yet, a strong-willed wife is a confident woman as well. This means she knows what she wants. If she is with you after many years, brother, count your blessings as one worthy to be with such a strong woman, because other men have fallen by the wayside after the initial "head butt."

GORILLA

As big and strong as the gorilla is, his male organ is ONLY three inches long. I believe every man would say that a gorilla is a very strong animal, but his procreation tool is quite small. However, he still commands respect.

Some husbands may feel the same way and have low self-esteem, but they do not have to. They can have the courage to see and love their wives to the best of their abilities. And there are more ways to having and making love. Men, in the end women are looking for men to sweep them off their feet in more ways than in the bed. Talk to your wife; she will tell you how.

Chapter 20:
Dealing with Truth

Be prepared to blow your wife away when you finally speak the truth. When you blow someone away, it takes time for him or her to recover. If you are not sympatric toward her feelings after telling your dark secret, she may never recover from your initial words.

Again, this separates the boys from the men. A man will tell the truth no matter what the circumstance. A boy will run away from speaking the truth. Again, men, you have dealt with this secret for a couple of years, and so you have gotten used to holding this thing close to your vest. But your wife had a notion but no clue about the specifics of your sexual issues.

Again, I say sexual secrets can be from orientation to the way YOU really like it in bed. For the sexual orientation, some MAJOR issues could dissolve the marriage. If you are having an affair, some MAJOR issues may affect the marriage. Everything else the wife may be able to bear. I say, maybe.

The reason why I say the other type of sexual secrets, sexual orientation and affairs, is because such sexual secrets (sins) deal with another person. When you are dealing with another person, whether live or by computer, you are possibly hurting the marriage beyond reconciliation.

Again, when you speak to your wife, do not look and feel so shocked. You must be her shock absorbers. I know this sounds old, but it still needs to be spoken.

Secrets can even cover up having a child by another woman that your wife does not know about.

Furthermore, what makes matters worse is when she asked you and you flat out lied to her. Brothers, if you lied a lot, what do you expect her to feel? She asks you the same question in many different ways, but you give the same answer every single time: NO.

So, by continually lying and now you tell the truth, how would you expect her to react? What if your wife lied to you continually about a subject you repeatedly asked about? I think that speaks volumes.

Chapter 21:
Wife's Perspective When Her Husband Tells the Truth

The manner in which a man speaks to his wife is very important, especially when he finally tells the truth about his bedroom secrets. He cannot come off as if she is forcing him to speak or come off in an arrogant way. These types of attitude issues will affect how the wife takes in the news that for some years the husband has been hiding or lying about. This is especially true for men who have been caught by their wives within their secrets. When a husband is caught, he should come out with his hands up. No attitude should be given, because, men, you have done something wrong and have deteriorated the marriage.

Men, a guilty party should show some form of regret. Yet, I have seen men do just the opposite and come out with blazing anger and resentment toward their wives. Your wife did not do this, sir, you did.

Again, men, you are dispelling your secret to her and when you do, you should do it with humility, not arrogance. And do not think this is the end of the conversation; it has just started in her mind. Which is why if your wife had patience with all of your lying, you should have patience with her healing. In addition, the healing process has no timetable or dynamics to it.

Husbands with secrets should not come out in a controlling way of how the wife should carry out the sensitive matter. Again, the guilty party rests on the mercy of the court and not the other way around.

Husbands who are guilty, be glad if your wife decides to deal with your mess after you confess. This is not a time to fling out your hormones. This is a time of weeping and repenting to your wife. And yes, expect her to have a trust issue.

Men who come off ugly are going down the wrong path to reconciliation. Your wife may take your mess, but you do not have to present your mess like it is the best thing since sliced bread, either. You have to come off as if you know this is a real and hurtful thing to her and understand for her this is another dent in your armor.

A man cannot come off as if he is still in control of the situation when he speaks the truth. Men, in reality, you have lost your control, respect, and trust from your wife. You cannot come off as if you are still the man, because, sir, you are not. You have lost what you have given your wife. Your job is to earn that respect and trust back. And this will take more than a weekend.

Giving your wife a take-it-or-leave-it attitude should not be introduced. That attitude is really for the wife to take and not you. Yes, I do believe in speaking the truth, but do it in love and mercy. Coming off as if you are still the man is hypocritical. Sir, when you reveal a sexual secret, you are not in the catbird seat. And coming off as if you are in control only strengthens her argument for leaving you instead of working things out.

For those who wonder why they should tell the truth and deal with all of these consequences, the answer is plain. The truth will set you free. The manner that you tell the truth will speak positive or negative volumes to your wife. Coming off like an idiot is not the way to go. Your job is to come in humility and restoration.

When your wife responds and she will, you, the husband, cannot have an attitude that says, "I should not have told you in the first place."

Your attitude should be, "I told you and I am a much better man for speaking the truth instead of a lie." You tell your wife the truth because you love her. If you hate her, you will keep the lie. But if you love her, you will speak the truth.

The manner of the wife's response is very important. A man wants his wife to respond in a loving way and have a lot of love for him for speaking the truth. He hopes that she will show him mercy for speaking the truth. This is what a husband wants, but reality and wants are two different things. A husband wants his wife to realize that he is finally telling her the truth about himself.

In reality, a man is speaking the truth without restrictions as in the Garden of Eden. A man must know that secrets will only kill the relationship in the end. Living a lie may be good for the man, but he has to get beyond his selfishness and give his wife the whole story.

Men, do not go to the grave with your lies. Some people may tell all, and others may not tell because they knew that the news will destroy their marriages. Yes, I know that, but that is the chance you take.

When you tell the truth, Christian married couples should have a level of forgiveness. However, men, that level of forgiveness does not necessarily mean she will stay with you. She will forgive you, but staying with you is a completely different matter. I hear some say, "What advantage is there in speaking the truth?"

I will tell you the great advantage is knowing that you have no more secrets to tell. Men, as you know, when you tell one lie you have to tell another one to keep up with the first one. If anything, men die from stress, stress because they have not revealed all to their spouses. Again, your wife may forgive you, but the damage may have been done. However, a true man can roll with the punches and still survive.

When R. Kelly did his song about the closet, there was a point of almost murder. Men, you must expect that when you come out she is apt to do anything. The consequence of telling the truth may not go in your favor.

Yet, it is liberating when you speak the truth. You are no longer bound by your sins and wrongs, because you have spoken them out. In nature, if you hold your breath, you will die, but if you let it go you will live. Live, my brothers, live. The truth will always outweigh the consequences.

Are there exceptions to telling the truth? In my opinion, the answer is no. Yet, there are men who are reading this book who have really messed up. This includes having another family that the present spouse knows nothing about. You may want to speak with a pastor or professional counselor to find out how to let it out.

And, men, the environment of you telling your wife is very important, too. Do not call Jerry Springer and ask to be on the show to spill the beans. You have to be in the right area and frame of mind to speak the truth with your wife.

No, you cannot dress up the secret, but the manner and place that you do it are as important. Why? Because your wife will remember that time and place forever. And that time and place will be forever stamped in her brain. So, if you tell her in a crappy place, that will go with the environment of you uncovering the truth. However, the opposite is possibly true if you choose an exotic location.

Telling your wife the truth during an argument is not a good time or place. You should choose your time and place to speak the truth. Just as you planned and hid your lie, you should take the same energy and find the place and time to let your wife know that you have been lying all these years.

In essence, you cannot tell her how to react to your secret. She has a right to react in any form that she desires. The reaction is up to her; your placement of the truth is on you. And when you speak, do not give out gray areas; tell it all. In my opinion, when you let it out one piece (or day) at a time it is no good. Give her all the bad news so that it is done and over with from the perspective of what was the lie. Dealing with the consequences may take a lifetime.

Dealing with sexual secrets is a two-part issue. Part one is revealing the secret, and part two is healing from it. Part two cannot happen until all of part one is complete. Until you tell all, part two will not take place, and a wife knows when more needs to come out of that situation. Do not ask me how; she just knows when there is more to spill.

When you "out" yourself, you had better have God in Christ on your side, because the road will be hard as you go through this journey, not just for your sake, but for your children's as well. I cannot over-emphasize this point to you. To deal with the secret, you need Christ in your life. Some believe and go to other points, but for my house and me, I believe God in Christ is the way to go and fight against your wrong, men. You need the support that comes from God and God alone.

Men, you violated God's laws, especially when it deals with adultery. So, does it not make sense to have God in your life to help you along the way? If you did this without God, does it not make sense to learn from your mistake and have God in your life now?

In my opinion, God in Christ is the way to go to fight and support yourself as you go through this journey. Hear me, men. Your wife will not be your support for a while because she is dealing with the truth.

On the flip side, a good wife will see her husband's heart and make a decision. And men, for her to make a positive decision toward you, you must make a STRONG COMMITMENT to her and God in Christ. Without this recommitment to her and God, you are probably doomed.

So, men, in essence, get straight with God and then with your wives.

Based on the secret, you may also want to get a professional third party involved. It may be expensive, but it may be a smart move. The key is the power of the secret in your life. If it can cause an issue, especially a domestic violence one, you may need a professional third party involved as you speak the truth.

Certain things your wife will not forgive you for, but God will, my brother. This is why you have to go to God first and get it right with him through God in Christ. You need God in this thing from beginning to end.

Chapter 22:
If You Can't Handle the Truth, Do Not Ask

Very simply put for all to see. If you cannot handle your husband speaking to you, then you need not ask, and ask God for grace. Wives, if your hearts are not ready, do not go down that path until you are ready to hear whatever your husband has to say to you. Many wives have gone crazy because they were not able to handle such truths from their husbands.

This is one dimension where wives go wrong: asking for an answer that they cannot handle. Granted, saying you are ready and being ready are two different things when it comes down to the point of pressing, but you did ask for it. If you are truly ready, then ask for it. Usually, ladies, you know you are ready when your gut tells you that something is wrong with your husband. However, just going by gossip is not a good reason. You have to prepare yourself for the worst when he speaks the truth. Yet, through the God in Christ, you will be able to make it through this transition from deceit to truth.

Wives, before you go down the path, make sure your facts are not emotional. You cannot go on thought; you must have the facts. In this, a husband cannot deny the truth. Remember, he lied this far, and he may lie again. By having all the cards on the table, he cannot run from the truth.

In essence, are you ready for the truth? Are you ready to make the decision that will affect your family forever? Yes, ladies, the ball is in your court when your husband spills the beans. The decision may be to stay, or your decision may be to leave. The only words I can give you is think hard on your decision before making it.

Also, know that your husband may NOT CHANGE. Can you deal with the truth about your husband? Do not get me wrong. If he has an adultery problem, I do not see a reason for you to stay. Yet, anything less than that is your decision. Whether you continue the relationship as long as he is telling the truth about it is your decision alone to make.

Do not make the decision because of the kids; make the decision because it is the best decision for you. As the children depended on you in your womb, they depend on you again to make the decision that is best for all.

Chapter 23:
Proverbs and Song of Solomon

The next few pages are scriptures from God's holy writ as relates to adultery, communication, and sex. I added this section because I believe that every man who NOW speaks the truth and makes the necessary adjustments needs guidance in going forward in the marriage. You cannot stay in a mind frame (secrets) and expect the same results.

The first part of this book encouraged men to come out of the secrets, yet when you come out, you need new skills. It took a skill to stay in the secret; well, it is going to take skills to stay

OUT of the secret. Hence, this is why the following scriptures are given to help you deal with this new environment called truth. The air is different in the closet versus outside the closet.

On some of the passages, I give detailed information to dig deep. On others, I give Hebrew root words to help bring out the scripture.

Read, learn and enjoy. All Hebrew translations comes from the *Hebrew Strong Concordance*.

HARLOT

Proverbs 7:10 -

And, behold, there met him a woman with the attire of a harlot, and subtle of heart.

The word harlot (zw-nawb 2180) in Hebrew means to commit adultery or idolatry. The word subtil (naw-tsar 5341) in Hebrew means to conceal, besiege, or hidden thing.

Every man must ask two questions. Is the woman you meet your wife, and two, how is she dressed? There is nothing wrong with a husband meeting a woman, but issues occur when she is 1) dressed like a harlot; and 2) has a deceitful heart.

Husbands, we must guard our hearts from women in harlot attire. Also, understand she may not be dressed in harlot attire but have a subtle heart. Men, we know the types who are always up to no good. These women always smile with a hidden agenda. In addition, men, we have to ensure that we do not encourage such behavior.

To fight this, husbands should ask their wives to wear clothes that are appealing to them. This request is not forced, but asked. Husbands must be real and tell their wives what they desire to see.

Yet, husbands must compromise and allow the wives to only wear such in non-public arenas if their wives so choose. However, if the wife and husband are into dressing sexy in public, have at it. Yet, if one of the spouses has envy DNA, I would not suggest sexy attire in public.

In total, a husband must judge a woman on her heart. Moreover, when her heart is out to catch and prey on another husband, one must run. As Joseph ran, so must men who meet such women. In final, some women are just looking for sugar daddies. Brothers, the only sugar daddy you should be is to the one with your last name.

These women know what men like to hear and see, and we who are committed to our wives must be smart to not fall into their traps. These women are like sour grapes: good for the look, but sour to the taste.

Harlot attire is simply anything that will cause your mind or penis to erect. Under no circumstance should men be around these women, because the more you talk to them, the harder the temptation becomes. The more you look at a live woman, the more you may want to taste. This includes even thinking about her over a long period.

All you need is at your home, brother.

Proverbs 29:3

- Whoso loveth wisdom rejoiceth his father: but he that keepeth company with harlots spendeth his substance.

The word company (raw-aw 7462) in Hebrew means to "associate with." The word spendeth (aw-bad 6) in Hebrew means to lose oneself, implication of perishing, break, destroy, to be undone, or nowhere to flee.

This scripture speaks for itself. When you deal with strange women, you are making a bad investment. A good man will leave an inheritance for his children. One cannot leave an inheritance if any portion is going toward a harlot or strange woman. In the end, his initial investment will cost him everything.

I do not know the going rate for harlots or Internet chat rooms, but I know things will add up. The money you spend on strange women will end up costing more, because after one bite you will continue.

A good decisive test, men, is can your wife at anytime examine your credit card or phone statements? If she cannot, then you are hiding, and hiding means great consequences in the end. As stated, truth is the ultimate decision every man will have to make. If you have to hide your sexual taboo or answer questions with lies, you are on a street called Stupid and Divorce.

I cannot get into the number of STDs hitting our homes. Again, the investment will add up over time. Yes, I hear men say, "Well, my wife will not do what this harlot or prostitute did." This may be true, husbands, but have you ever asked why she has not done so and so?

The key is to talk with your wife until you reach a compromise. And no, the compromise should not include seeing a harlot on a scheduled basis. I know some wives have been so hurt that they do not even care. At this point, a wife obligates the man to find answers. This should turn a man into a physician to heal the wounds of his wife to change this attitude.

These harlots also include male prostitutes. Both are wrong and adultery. Did you read the Hebrew translation of spending? Powerful but true when it says it implicates destruction to the home. Anything that makes you move away from your wife is a problem. If you never touch your wife due to sexual taboos, you cannot be right. Or if you hide your sexual taboos, you are just as wrong.

Men, for the sake of your kids, do not bring a fatal attraction to your home. You may pay for it with your life.

WOMEN

Proverbs 22:14 -

The mouth of strange women is a deep pit: he that is abhorred of the LORD shall fall therein.

The word mouth (peh 6310) in Hebrew means to "speech." The word abhorred (zaw-am 2194) in Hebrew means to have indignation and be angry.

The deep pit is a chasm so deep that it is going to take a lot to get you out. To avoid the pit, you must go around it. If you think you can get out of the pit on your own, you are living in a dream world. A pit takes you away from your FAMILY. More importantly, when you fall into a pit, no one knows where you are but God and you. When you are married, it is no longer just you; it is you and your spouse. And if you are in a pit, she needs to know. This again goes back to the importance of not having secrets within the marriage.

From God's perspective, He hates this. Going into another house is having adultery. No matter how you cut it, you are still having an affair, and God commands that those who go after strange women will fall therein.

You cannot keep looking over a chasm and not fall in. Many men just looked too long at another woman and fell into a hole. As men, we are surrounded by images of beautiful women. You do not have to look at *Playboy* to see that. Yet, for all men, we must not follow such women into their pits. As the song says, you have to let them "walk on by." If you let them walk by, you are not in trouble. However, if you follow, you will end up in a pit.

In addition, do not take your issues to another woman. Your issue must be completed with your wife and your wife alone.

Proverbs 23:33 -

Thine eyes shall behold strange women, and thine heart shall utter perverse things.

The word eyes (ahyin 5869) in Hebrew means

"outward appearance." The word things (tah-poo-kaw- 8419) in Hebrew means fraud.

The problem with looking is that you do not know what you are getting until you bite. Most men who have had affairs will agree that the affair was not worth the loss of family and name. Oh yeah, she looked fine, but the deeper the man looked, the more he discovered a tormented woman who only used her body for self-gratification. In other words, the house was built, but no one was home.

The Hebrew translation gives great insight into this passage. As men, we must stay grounded and not let our penis get the best of us. One problem I have is that the church only talks about the dangers of one aspect of sexual taboos, but there are other dangers that if a man is not looking, he will be hit without knowledge.

If men would be honest, danger is everywhere; it all depends on how you react to the danger. When the conditions are dangerous, you put on protection to eliminate the risk. No, husbands, I am not talking about using a condom with a prostitute. I am talking about avoiding the dangers that are around and taking appropriate actions. If you cannot handle the danger, move to a safe haven.

This is true after an argument. After a fight, your

mind is more moved to look, and these are the times you must be strong and careful. A smart wife will never let her husband leave mad or upset to work. To him, work may reflect other options. I am not saying he is justified, I am just stating the facts.

What you see, my brothers, is not what you get. I believe if men would fast-forward to their lust conclusion with another woman or chat rooms, they would have a different mind frame. In fact, before you use your sight, use your heart. Many men use the eyes instead of the heart. Many men use the penis instead of the heart before making decisions. Men, do not ONLY look. Think.

Proverbs 31:3 -

Give not thy strength unto women, nor thy ways to that which destroyeth kings.

Strength in the Hebrew translation is hayil (2428) which means valor, wealth, and virtue. Destroyeth in Hebrew translates to mahah (4229), which means to erase.

I think this scripture tells us the dangers of following a strange woman. A strange woman is so powerful that she can destroy or erase a king. I do not know how many natural kings are reading this book, but if a strange woman can destroy a king, what can she do to a non-king (husband)?

The scripture should add a "strange" woman and not just a woman, because in essence you give yourself to your wife as she does to you. This is the submitting that God commands both husbands and wives to do.

Most men have the Samson factor. The factor says that a man will give himself to somebody in his lifetime. And the person to whom he gives it to will either be his killer or supporter. In essence, the fault is not the woman but the man, because he decides whom to marry.

Again, men who leave their wives for women they meet over the Internet are wrong. The point is staying faithful. Do not let your eyes or penis destroy you.

Proverbs 2:16 -

To deliver thee from the strange woman, even from the stranger which flattereth with her words;

Deliver (5337) means to snatch away. Flattereth (2505) means to smooth.

Like any rock, if you have enough water, you can smooth away the stone. Men, we must be on guard for the "watery" women who come out to snatch us away from our anointing and family. Countless men have fallen victim to such tactics. We, as men, must learn from other mistakes and not repeat them.

We need God to help us stay faithful to our wives. As a man and preacher, I have become realistic. In that, I mean I know as men we are not going to be perfect, and our wives must know WE will HAVE dents in our armor. Yet, we must be honest and trustful with our wives about our sexual struggles.

I believe, short of any form of adultery with another woman, a loving wife should be able to handle your faults or sexual taboos. Yet, if she cannot, you'd rather she leave you for truth than for lies.

Another point is when you are having a bad day run from any woman who gives flattereth words, because just one comment can take you down her road. In addition, her road only leads to destruction. Do not be bullheaded and say you can handle it. Many married graves are written with the epitaph of: "**He thought he could handle it, but instead it handled him**."

Proverbs 5:3 -

For the lips of a strange woman drop as a

honeycomb, and her mouth is smoother than oil:

Honeycomb (5317) in Hebrew means shaking to pieces and a dripping.

Although the scriptures seem repetitive, most of us must be aware of the lips. Honeycomb means a shaking to pieces. For me, this means one being moved from one set of values to another set.

Adultery, no matter how Hollywood dresses it up, is still a fly in the ointment of love between two married individuals. Though I know a woman can also have an affair, the point of example must come from the man. So, men, lead the way and restrain yourself as you deal with the opposite sex. The taste may be sweet, but the results are surely bitter.

Proverbs 5:5 -

Her feet go down to death; her steps take hold on hell.

Proverbs 5:20 -

And why wilt thou, my son, be ravished with a strange woman, and embrace the bosom of a stranger?

Ravished (7686) means to stray, mistake, or element of intoxication. Looking is one thing, but touching is a whole other element. The point of the matter is embracing the strange woman in your bosom. This can be done mentally or physically. In all, this dance is dangerous, and no one wins.

When you touch the drink and take another one, you are being taken down a well that is quite deep. One drink after another will do the trick. Many men who are reading this are guilty of taking the first sip of a strange woman. Once you do, you are in danger, because you just cannot have just one, you must have many sips. And, in life, when you drink more than one drink, you are going to get drunk.

When you are drunk with lust, your judgment is impaired. The only way to stop the "drinking" with a strange woman is to stop cold turkey and find your wife with love. Your marriage may not be perfect, but why mess with it? If you are going down the journey of life, why complicate it with a strange woman?

I do not know, but when something is called strange, it means you are not sure of its effects. In addition, strange means something that is not normal. Yes, my brother, it is not normal for you to take another man's wife. It is not normal for you to go to a place that is not your own home.

The strange woman is not the problem; it is you.

A woman can do what only a man allows her to do. So, men, do not blame the short dress or sexy attire. You are the man who must make the change for the sake of your family and reputation. What you do in the privacy of your home is cool, as long as it is not illegal and kept a secret among heterosexual married partners.

I heard one person talk about one sexual taboo as wrong, but another sexual taboo they did not touch because they were guilty of it. Let us solve this problem now. All have sinned and come short of the glory of God. One sin is not greater than the other.

Brothers, please, I am not trying to get into your business, but when you bring home a live strange woman into your home by contact (verbal and physical), you are letting a foreign object or strange woman mess up your home. Beware, men, beware. When I say live, I mean you can physically touch or talk to her. Many are infatuated, but the key is to not turn it into covetousness or reality. When it becomes emotional or reality, it becomes adultery.

Proverbs 6:24 -

To keep thee from the evil woman, from the flattery of the tongue of a strange woman.

Proverbs 6:26 -

For by means of a whorish woman a man is brought to a piece of bread: and the adulteress will hunt for the precious life.

Men, your marriage is precious. We are a dying breed in our American culture. Not too many men are faithfully married to one woman. To ward off the strange woman, we must look at our marriage as precious. For those who have gone through a divorce, the point is quite expensive. It costs a lot of money to go your separate ways. Again, this is why the Bible calls your life precious in the life and mind of your marriage.

However, the key I want to focus on is hunt. Hunt (6679) means to lie alongside and take. You do not have to look; they will come looking for you. This is why men have to fight the spirit of not being appreciated. As men, we go through this phase in our lives. And when we do this, the adulteress is on the hunt.

Men, our job is not to get caught in the net. The net of a strange woman brings nothing but captivity and shame into our lives. I am not saying you will be perfect in all things. However, I am saying that when you let yourself become a victim of an adulteress, you have spelled the death of your family.

Proverbs 6:32 -

But whoso committeth adultery with a woman lacketh understanding: he that doeth it destroyeth his own soul.

Proverbs 7:27 -

Her house is the way to hell, going down to the chambers of death.

Proverbs 9:13 -

A foolish woman is clamorous: she is simple, and knoweth nothing.

Even though Solomon is talking about women, men are airheads, too. When you let your penis do all the thinking, you are an airhead. You do not see the danger that awaits you down the road. If a woman is simple, then it takes a simpler man to fall for it. Again, I cannot put the blame all on the woman. The man has a responsibility to say NO.

A clamorous (1993) means to make a loud sound and that is you falling because you followed a strange woman. Do not let that fall happen in your life. Can you imagine that after the affair people will point to your simple decision as the downfall of where you were going within your life?

If I am to be taken out, do not let a simple thing do it. I want to go out doing something hard and difficult. I say to all men, when you let a foolish woman take you away from your wife, you are just as simple. Be strong, men, be strong.

Proverbs 11:16 -

A gracious woman retaineth honour: and strong men retain riches.

Some men do not know that they have great wives until they are gone. As men, we need to count the full cost when entertaining an affair. In my humble mind, an affair never adds up.

Some just entertain and count the cost for the sexual fling, and they stop there. However, the smart one will count the cost not only in the natural but also in the spiritual. And any common man will say that an affair does not equal any great or long satisfaction.

Overall, a man needs to marry a woman who is gracious and keeps honor. This is why dating a woman is important. You need to see if her value increases. This goes for you, too, sir. Some rush to the altar without evaluating. And when I say evaluate, I do not mean from a sexual point of view. You must see if this is the kind of woman for you. Again, this is why the Bible says fornication is wrong because sex will complicate two individuals in making the correct decision.

In short, having two Christians dating does not mean an automatic click for marriage. It takes time to wade through the process before the eternal commitment is complete. I have seen couples who were saved go down to the altar, and in the end, it was a bad decision. Again, the value increases and does not decrease.

Proverbs 11:22 -

As a jewel of gold in a swine's snout, so is a fair woman, which is without discretion.

This may not come out right, but the key is, I do not care how fine a woman is; if she has no discretion, the word is run. Because men are eyes and penis conscious, and sometimes it is more powerful than our emotional consciousness, and we must ensure that we do not go based on what we see. It is not what you see; it is really what you get.

Men who are single, you must push past the glamour and gold, and discover what is on the inside of that woman. And no, I am not speaking sexually. Even, God forbid, if you are having sex with a woman, does she have discretion? Discretion (2940) means perception and intelligence.

Sex outside of marriage is wrong, because it lacks commitment. If you can have a contract for a car and a house payment, why can't you have one for the woman you love? If you can have a commitment letter for a credit card and other financial points, how much more is a wife worth? The Bible says that her price is above rubies. So, my logic is clear. If you have contracts for worldly things, why not have a contract (marriage) between you and your wife?

Men, you do not want to marry an airhead. You want a woman who can think for herself and will challenge you in the right way. This is important, because just in case God takes you home first, can she keep the business and family going? If you just marry a sex slave, you have spelled and written your own downfall. You want a woman who will deal with it all (spiritually, emotionally, sexually, and intelligently). This is not in order by importance but opportunity.

Yes, when you look for the total package understand, you will get more in some areas and less in others. The key is getting a woman who will have a little bit of all. Yes, men, I know we desire sex, but sex is not everything. We want it to be everything, but it is not, and you must date or stay married accordingly. Only a fool will jeopardize what he has tried hard to work for.

Proverbs 12:4 -

A virtuous woman is a crown to her husband:

but she that maketh ashamed is as rottenness in his bones.

Proverbs 14:1

Every wise woman buildeth her house: but the foolish plucketh it down with her hands.

You cannot make this plainer, as it relates to both sexes in a marriage. Although Solomon is speaking to the woman, we also know that a man can destroy his marriage, especially when he has committed adultery.

That is why a nagging spouse initiates an exploding bomb in the home. Once he bomb explodes, problems from past, present, and future will be displayed. Foolish spouses will destroy the house. Sometimes it is both, and other times it is one of the spouses. The key is that somebody has to be civil and ensure that the house is not destroyed. How dumb is it to get your point across but in the process you destroy the home? You got your point, but you have no home to house the point.

In all, no one can blame another because the house falls from within and not without. The scripture says that it will be plucked down with one's own hands. Let me ask a simple but powerful question: What have your hands done lately? Have your hands helped or destroyed the marriage? It is either one or the other, for it cannot be both.

Proverbs 21:9 -

It is better to dwell in a corner of the housetop, than with a brawling woman in a wide house.

In digging a little deeper, you will see that the Hebrew housetop comes from (1342) ga'ah, which means to rise. When your wife is coming after you, it does not necessarily mean to get away. It means to rise above the occasion of your wife and go higher than her.

In essence, due to maybe your actions, she is talking 'out of her head' toward you. When you are in this point in your mind, go to another level of thinking and act accordingly. So, when you wives are brawling, brothers, you cannot go to their level. You must remain or go even higher. Any man will attest to what happens when you battle a woman through communication. It will either make it worse or make you more upset.

Husbands, we must try to understand the source of their anger. If you are just fighting the fire, you are losing the battle. However, the smart one finds the source and shuts it off. Men, this is our job. Most men like to figure out things. Well, men, we need to apply these skills to our wives when they are in such a brawling manner toward us.

Unless a woman is possessed with the devil, she will not get mad for nothing. Something starts the process. The match of the fire is what we have to find, men. And be encouraged, because if she is brawling, she will not be so quick to tell you why she is so upset. But be patient and consistent, men. Do not give up, keep digging. Digging solves the problem and tells your wife how much you truly love her.

Proverbs 21:19

It is better to dwell in the wilderness, than with a contentious and an angry woman.

No Hebrew is needed here. Just know your wife's hot buttons, stand clear of them, and try to make peace with her as soon as possible. Solomon says it is better to go to the wilderness than deal with an angry woman. The key, however, is not that she is angry, but why she is angry and contentious. Have I done anything to her or has another done anything to her to make her feel this way?

As men, we are good in seeing the problem with our wives; we need to go to the next level, which is the WHEN, WHAT, WHERE, and HOW. Since most women are not psycho, there must be a kickoff to their anger. Your job is to find it and shut it down.

Proverbs 23:27 -

For a whore is a deep ditch; and a strange woman is a narrow pit.

Proverbs 27:15 -

A continual dropping in a very rainy day and a contentious woman are alike.

Wives, take note that when you keep talking after a period, the Bible calls you a contentious woman. The word contentious means a brawling woman, one who likes to fight and keep things going. The main question for men to answer is: Was she this way before I met her? If the answer is no, then it is on you, sir, to untangle this web within your wife with the help of God in Christ.

Most wives do this because they want attention for the problems in their lives. Women, as great as they are in talking, when it comes to negative things we do to them, they are not that great in direct communication. They will sometimes beat around the bush until you finally ask the right question to get the right answer to why they are acting a certain way. So, in essence, if you want to stop the dripping, you've got to turn the faucet off.

Proverbs 30:20 -

Such is the way of an adulterous woman; she eateth, and wipeth her mouth, and saith, I have done no wickedness.

Proverbs 30:21,23 -

For three things, the earth is disquieted, and for four which it can not bear. / For an odious woman when she is married; and an handmaid that is heir to her mistress.

Odious means to hate or one to be an enemy (H8130). In other words, she is unloved and unpleasant. Men who are single or engaged, if you have a woman like this, you might want to rethink that step according to this scripture. If again you are dating a woman who is always mad at either you or the world, you might want to clear it up before you walk down the point to the altar.

As it relates to men who are married with an unpleasant woman, your job is to investigate why. Just being mad at her for her statements and attitude is not enough. You must try to pry past her anger and find out why she is that way. Why does she feel a certain way toward you and life? In point, such actions will also affect the kids down the road if it continues.

Proverbs 31:10 -

Who can find a virtuous woman? for her price

is far above rubies.

This is one of the most popular scriptures about a good woman; the point is clear that a great woman is worth more than rubies or what the world offers. Again, this is why getting with a strange woman is stupid. She has no values. And when no values get close to a value (man), it will equal zero.

In other words, if you get close to a woman who is strange, she will bring down your value of life. There is no upswing. You may swing for a while, but the result is not worth the feeling you will have overall.

The key, men, is to find. The key is not her finding you, but you finding her. If you do not find her, you are not looking hard enough. If you look hard enough, you will find your blessing in the form of a woman. But you've got to look. Men who are single, let me say that where you look is what you will find in life. If you look in bad areas, you will find bad women.

Proverbs 31:30 -

Favour is deceitful, and beauty is vain: but a woman that feareth the LORD, she shall be praised.

HUSBAND

Proverbs 12:4 -

A virtuous woman is a crown to her husband: but she that maketh ashamed is as rottenness in his bones.

Proverbs 31:11 -

The heart of her husband doth safely trust in her, so that he shall have no need of spoil.

Proverbs 31:23

Her husband is known in the gates, when he sitteth among the elders of the land.

Proverbs 31:28 -

Her children arise up, and call her blessed; her husband also, and he praiseth her.

As you desire praise, so does your wife. Whatever you want from your wife, you should be the first partaker of it. If you want praise, give her praise first. Too many men make the mistake of not honoring their wives until it is too late. Sir, let this not be your point of conclusion.

I know she is not perfect, but guess what? You are not perfect, either. As she takes your dents, you must take hers. As she takes your imperfections, you must take hers. Yet, if you meditate only on the bad, you will lose out.

Make a conscious decision to meditate on the good within your life.

LIPS OR MOUTH

Proverbs 4:24 -

Put away from thee a forward mouth, and perverse lips put far from thee.

A forward mouth is one who is false and has dishonest speech. When you speak with untruth, you will live in untruth. You must be careful how you speak to your wife. If you cannot speak truth, do not speak at all. The word of God speaks clearly, that you must keep these things far from your relationship.

Proverbs 7:21 -

With her much fair speech she caused him to yield, with the flattering of her lips she forced him.

When she forces him, she makes him rethink his conscience and values. ANYTHING that makes you rethink your values is a wrong point. If you continue to let a woman feed you, you will leave your table of sense and go to a table of non-sense.

It is not looking at her lips but the point of what she means behind her lips. Many men are not aware of the dangers until it is too late. The key is if you are attracted to her, you must take note and go another way in life. The more you talk to her, the more you may leave your wife.

Affairs start emotionally, not physically. When you flirt, you started a problem that is deadly to your marriage.

Proverbs 12:22 -

Lying lips are abomination to the LORD: but they that deal truly are His delight.

An abomination is another level for sin, and lying lips will take you there. Notice in the Bible that adultery and fornication are not abominations, but lying lips are.

This again is why a smart man must speak the truth. When you keep lying to your wife, you are committing an abomination. I think if men could look at their conversation and imagine God right near their ear, they would do things differently. The point of mind is that no one can make you lie but you.

Proverbs 13:3 -

He that keepeth his mouth keepeth his life: but he that openeth wide his lips shall have destruction.

Proverbs 14:7 -

Go from the presence of a foolish man, when thou perceivest not in him the lips of knowledge.

Proverbs 16:13 -

Righteous lips are the delight of kings; and they love him that speaketh right.

Proverbs 16:27 -

An ungodly man diggeth up evil; and in his lips there is as a burning fire.

Proverbs 17:4 -

A wicked doer giveth heed to false lips; and a liar giveth ear to a naughty tongue.

Proverbs 17:28 -

Even a fool, when he holdeth his peace, is counted wise; and he that shutteth his lips is esteemed a man of understanding.

It is better to shut your mouth than to speak when you are not sure of what to say. Remember, it is better to keep silent than to misspeak. When you control your mouth, you are a man of understanding and wisdom. One point of wisdom is that a strong man is able to control his tongue and not let his tongue control him.

Proverbs 18:6 -

A fool's lips enter into contention, and his mouth calleth for strokes.

Proverbs 27:2 -

Let another man praise thee, and not thine own mouth; a stranger, and not thine own lips.

Proverbs 6:2 -

Thou art snared with the words of thy mouth; thou art taken with the words of thy mouth.

In the scheme of things, the only person who can get you in trouble is you. This word from the holy writ makes this known in full that your words can dig your grave. Men, overall we must be careful of the words we speak to our wives. One thing over time that men must know is that whatever you say to your wife, she WILL PROCESS.

Our mouths snare us. Whatever we speak, our wives will take into consideration. The words that I speak will have a lasting effect.

Proverbs 8:7 -

For my mouth shall speak truth; and

wickedness is an abomination to my lips.

Proverbs 13:3 -

He that keepeth his mouth keepeth his life: but he that openeth wide his lips shall have destruction.

Proverbs 15:14 -

The heart of him that hath understanding seeketh knowledge; but the mouth of fools feedeth on foolishness.

You cannot keep listening to garbage and expect your marriage to survive. Negative in will create negative out. One who understands that stops the foolishness. This is especially true of those who listen to friends and relatives who have bad marriages themselves, but have all the answers despite being on marriage four.

The point I am trying to make is that when you feed on garbage, you become a garbage can.

Proverbs 15:23 -

A man hath joy by the answer of his mouth; and a word spoken in due season, how good is it!

Proverbs 15:28 -

The heart of the righteous studieth to answer, but the mouth of the wicked poureth out evil things.

The scripture is clear that a wise person will study his answer. Husbands and wives will not rush through an answer. Since your life is based on your spouse, it would make sense to take time and speak well to your spouse.

When you speak quickly, you may cause a problem down the road that could spell defeat. So, study your answer. For the person who asks the question, this shows the value you have in them. When you do a forced answer, the person who asked understands that you did not give him or her proper respect by answering like a fool or person who has no true interest. As you study life, study your answer. In doing so, you have fewer mistakes to erase.

Proverbs 18:7 -

A fool's mouth is his destruction, and his lips are the snare of his soul.

Proverbs 18:20 -

A man's belly shall be satisfied with the fruit of his mouth; and with the increase of his lips shall he be filled.

Proverbs 21:23 -

Whoso keepeth his mouth and his tongue keepeth his soul from troubles.

Proverbs 30:32 -

If thou hast done foolishly in lifting up thyself, or if thou hast thought evil, lay thine hand upon thy mouth.

This should be a new sign to all couples when they have made a mistake. When you speak too soon, you lose out. Instead of fighting about it, the guilty party should just put his hand over his mouth and be done with it. And before he puts his hands over his mouth, he should recite Proverbs 30:32.

BREAST

This section is solely for letting people know that it is all right to talk erotic to your married spouse. The beauty that God has given should not inhibit. Since there is no marriage or given in marriage in heaven, you might want to enjoy it on this Earth with the person with whom you have a marriage license.

Enjoy and recite back to your spouse.

Proverbs 5:19 -

Let her be as the loving hind and pleasant roe; let her breasts satisfy thee at all times; and be thou ravished always with her love.

The major issue in this verse, men, is not to ONLY focus on that part of her body. Your wife is not a walking breast or vagina. We are, however, a walking penis, but your wife is not a walking sex organ.

Meaning that when you do touch, do not go crazy with it. When you do, she feels like a piece of meat and not your wife. Therefore, husbands, pace yourself. Just as it is rude to devour your food in ten minutes, the same is said toward your wife. Examine other aspects of your wife's body.

Wives, you have to show your husband some skin. If you run into the bedroom and cover yourself up quickly, you are not working toward a strong marriage. In fact, you are working toward your husband finding other things to look at.

If your husband is a greedy newborn baby who loves to touch and feel the breast, you've got to train him just like your trained your newborn.

Let him know the kinder he is, the more he can examine. Some men do not believe that the vagina and breast are attached to your body. Some men are just rude when it comes to the female body. Wife, train him to love you; he wants to learn.

Song of Solomon Chapter 1

2 Let him kiss me with the kisses of his mouth-- for your love is more delightful than wine.

3 Pleasing is the fragrance of your perfumes; your name is like perfume poured out. No wonder the maidens love you!

10 Your cheeks are beautiful with earrings, your neck with strings of jewels.

12 While the king was at his table, my perfume spread its fragrance.

13 My lover is to me a sachet of myrrh resting between my breasts.

In antiquity, women used to wear pouches of perfume around their necks. In other words, there was a draw to the area. Wives, you ought to smell good. Husbands, you ought to smell good as well.

This was also done to enhance sexual pleasure and attractiveness. What is wrong with us as Christians who do not try to be attractive toward our mates? This scripture tells couples to do things that will make them sexual toward each other.

Do not fool yourself. When you become a Christian, desires of "being wanted" do not go away. You have to understand that Christ changes you, but nature is nature. When couples stop wanting each other, problems are surely to abound.

If you use species for food, how much more for the human body as it relates to sexuality?

14 My lover is to me a cluster of henna blossoms from the vineyards of En Gedi.

En Gedi was an oasis in the Middle East area. It was a place of rest in the midst of a desert. This is what good sex is between two married heterosexual persons. It is a place of refreshing. It is a place of great blessing, because here is where you let the power flow between the two.

May I add, some frustrations occur in the home because there is no sexual release. I have said it before; the Lord has given us this sexual organ for a reason. It is not just to procreate. It is to be enjoyed between two married individuals.

15 How beautiful you are, my darling! Oh, how beautiful! Your eyes are doves.

16 How handsome you are, my lover! Oh, how charming! And our bed is verdant.

Song of Solomon 2

1 I am a rose of Sharon, a lily of the valleys.

5 Strengthen me with raisins, refresh me with apples, for I am faint with love.

6 His left arm is under my head, and his right arm embraces me.

7 Daughters of Jerusalem, I charge you by the gazelles and by the does of the field; do not arouse or awaken love until it so desires.

13 The fig tree forms its early fruit; the blossoming vines spread their fragrance. Arise, come, my darling; my beautiful one, come with me.

14 My dove in the clefts of the rock, in the hiding places on the mountainside, show me your face, let me hear your voice; for your voice is sweet, and your face is lovely.

16 My lover is mine and I am his; he browses among the lilies.

Song of Solomon 3

2 I will get up now and go about the city, through its streets and squares; I will search for the one my heart loves. So I looked for him but did not find him.

Song of Solomon 4

1 How beautiful you are, my darling! Oh, how beautiful! Your eyes behind your veil are doves. Your hair is like a flock of goats descending from Mount Gilead.

2 Your teeth are like a flock of sheep just shorn, coming up from the washing. Each has its twin; not one of them is alone.

3 Your lips are like a scarlet ribbon; your mouth is lovely. Your temples behind your veil are like the halves of a pomegranate.

4 Your neck is like the tower of David, built with elegance; on it hang a thousand shields, all of them shields of warriors.

5 Your two breasts are like two fawns, like twin fawns of a gazelle that browse among the lilies.

6 Until the day breaks and the shadows flee, I will go to the mountain of myrrh and to the hill of incense.

7 All beautiful you are, my darling; there is no flaw in you.

9 You have stolen my heart, my sister, my bride; you have stolen my heart with one glance of your eyes, with one jewel of your necklace.

10 How delightful is your love, my sister, my bride! How much more pleasing is your love than wine, and the fragrance of your perfume than any spice!

11 Your lips drop sweetness as the honeycomb, my bride; milk and honey are under your tongue. The fragrance of your garments is like that of Lebanon.

Song of Solomon 5

2 I slept but my heart was awake. Listen! My lover is knocking: "Open to me, my sister, my darling, my dove, my flawless one. My head is drenched with dew, my hair with the dampness of the night."

5 I arose to open for my lover, and my hands dripped with myrrh, my fingers with flowing myrrh, on the handles of the lock.

11 His head is purest gold; his hair is wavy and black as a raven.

12 His eyes are like doves by the water streams, washed in milk, mounted like jewels.

13 His cheeks are like beds of spice yielding perfume. His lips are like lilies dripping with myrrh.

14 His arms are rods of gold set with chrysolite. His body is like polished ivory decorated with

sapphires.

15 His legs are pillars of marble set on bases of pure gold. His appearance is like Lebanon, choice as its cedars.

16 His mouth is sweetness itself; he is altogether lovely. This is my lover, this my friend, O daughters of Jerusalem.

Song of Solomon 6

6 Your teeth are like a flock of sheep coming up from the washing. Each has its twin, not one of them is alone.

7 Your temples behind your veil are like the halves of a pomegranate.

9 But my dove, my perfect one, is unique, the only daughter of her mother, the favorite of the one who bore her. The maidens saw her and called her blessed; the queens and concubines praised her.

Song of Solomon 7

Song of Solomon Chapter 7 is from the NIV version.

There are sixteen references to body parts in this chapter. And it seems plain that Solomon was a breast man, too. Solomon was going after a woman for his harem.

If the Bible can give us such language, why does the church have problems in letting husbands and wives talk to each other in the most intimate and erotic detail? Couples, let go of the chains of legalism and begin the courtship of a lifetime. Enjoy this portion of scripture from Songs of Solomon Chapter 7:

1 How beautiful your sandaled feet, O prince's daughter! Your graceful legs are like jewels, the work of a craftsman's hands.

2 Your navel is a rounded goblet that never lacks blended wine. Your waist is a mound of wheat encircled by lilies.

3 Your breasts are like two fawns, twins of a gazelle.

4 Your neck is like an ivory tower. Your eyes are the pools of Heshbon by the gate of Bath Rabbim. Your nose is like the tower of Lebanon looking toward Damascus.

5 Your head crowns you like Mount Carmel. Your hair is like royal tapestry; the king is held captive by its tresses.

6 How beautiful you are and how pleasing, O love, with your delights!

7 Your stature is like that of the palm, and your breasts like clusters of fruit.

8 I said, "I will climb the palm tree; I will take hold of its fruit." May your breasts be like the clusters of the vine, the fragrance of your breath like apples,

9 and your mouth like the best wine.

10 I belong to my lover, and his desire is for me.

12 Let us go early to the vineyards to see if the vines have budded, if their blossoms have opened and if the pomegranates are in bloom.

Song of Solomon 8

4 Daughters of Jerusalem, I charge you: Do not arouse or awaken love until it so desires.

7 Many waters cannot quench love; rivers cannot wash it away. If one were to give all the wealth of his house for love, it would be utterly scorned.

10 I am a wall, and my breasts are like towers. Thus I have become in his eyes like one bringing contentment.

14 Come away, my lover, and be like a gazelle or like a young stag on the spice-laden mountains.

In total, I hope you were blessed by the rediscovery of erotic scripture. Although Solomon was using his words to add to his harem, there are points we can take within our married bedrooms. Especially the point of not being afraid to speak in erotic tones.

God created sex for married persons, yet due to points of ignorance, the church has missed out on something that was created and birthed for them. Solomon teaches husbands how to relate and talk to their wives.

A point of concern is never compare your wife to another woman. Though Solomon compared this woman to other animals and figures, all is well as long as he did not compare her to another woman.

Men who are running away from the secret: I am speaking to you to dissipate complications down the road, including comparing your wife to another. In essence, you are recovering from the points of your secrets; do not add to the problem by comparing her to other female individuals.

This section above just gave men pointers on how to speak to their wives in a loving way. In speaking to your wife, you give her what she desires, which is communication. The more you give her of communication, the more she will give you. In your recovery time with your wife, you will need a lot of communication with her to keep the marriage. Yet when opportunity comes, give her love talk. This will not happen overnight, but in your explaining, repenting, and confessing, she still needs a lot of loving and sex talk. She may not have sex with you because she is hurt, but letting her know you want and desire her will not be missed in the end.

Conclusion

The book is quite simple in helping men uncover their sexual secrets. Sin is sin and it will be judged, yet one should not have secrets from their married spouse. Though this book spoke primarily at times on homosexuality, the fact remains if a spouse is doing something sexually that the other spouse know not of, it is wrong.

Adam and Eve were completely naked in the garden. In my book, this means there were no secrets. Secrets can kill. With affairs, down low activity, and other things, couples are not only divorcing, but dying, because one spouse hid a sexual secret from the other.

I pray this book would get you closer to God in Christ as well as strengthen your relationship with your spouse.

For the men who are reading this book, I pray you destroy your secret. Be man enough to reveal yourself truly to your wife. Again, this book was not just for men wrestling with their identity; it was for all men who have sexual secrets from their wives.

On no terms should there be secrets between you and your spouse. Destroy the closet, men. Every time you buy a piece of "wood," destroy it quickly, because you will start to rebuild again if not careful.

Men, as we conclude this book, I advise you to put all your cards on the table. One thing that a woman wants more than anything is an honest man, a man who will tell her the truth even if the truth is ugly and dark.

A wife may want to make love in the dark, but not walk with her husband in the dark. This is unfair to the both of you. I advise you before you marry her to write down your sins and ask her to do the same. A powerful kick-off to a great marriage is honesty.

Have you ever seen a mountain climber? His or her next step could be the last. May I say without hesitation that when you enter a relationship, make every step count, because it could be your last. And remember the mountain fall is more dangerous than the mountain air. Climbing up the mountain is easier than falling from it.

In essence, when you lie to your woman, you are taking false steps that will eventually cause a fall that not only will hurt you but generations to come. Take the journey of honesty and put the cards on the table.

Before you get serious, before you walk down the aisle, let her know who you are by confessing your wrongs. Your call is to be honest and forthright. It has never been what the woman does. It has always been what the man does, because we are seen as the covering and leader of our home.

If it takes all year, do not become serious with her until she knows you by your sin. Why? Well, because when you and your love understand the limitations, you can then know your strengths.

When a firefighter goes in and fights a fire, he does not run in before he understands the weak points of the building. The same thing is applicable in your marriage. By you both knowing weak points, you are able to fight the fires together.

Hear me, my brother. I know showing your cards is a hard thing, but you have to do it. Be strong in the Lord and the power of His might.

As a woman births a baby, so must we as husbands birth truth in us. I say birth because it is so hard for us to speak the truth continually to our wives. Men have grown up with a mind frame that says get the woman by any means necessary. And, after marriage, we continue the mind frame of lying to get to our wives. We must birth truth, men.

Birthing is not for wimps; it is a hard task to perform. When men do not birth the baby of integrity, the marriage is affected for a lifetime. As a baby in the womb makes a wife uncomfortable, so does truth within your belly, sir. Having a baby makes you bigger and bloated, yet all these changes are necessary to birth a child. Well, sir, you are getting ready to walk in truth and honesty, but lifetime changes are going to be needed.

Men who are coming clean: you must understand your wife will have resentment toward you.

If you are man enough to make the storm, be man enough to deal with the storm. Hurricanes come out of the tropics where there is warm water, and due to pressure a hurricane is created.

Men, you must realize that your actions and secrets have created the "Hurricane." You must deal with the issues that lie ahead.

You cannot take her actions of wrath personally because you created it with your lying and secrets. This is good to understand when the storm starts to blow in your life. This is not to discourage you about its reality. My brothers, deal with the storm and get through it. Let your love be the bands that tie you to her when she acts up or has a flashback of your former life. God forgives and forgets, but your wife ain't God.

As time goes by, the storm will subside but how you act during the storm will only preclude how she will act the next time the storm is brewed. Hurricanes are fast and dangerous. So is the anger of your wife. But remember you caused it. Yet, your love, patience, understanding, and answering of questions will help you get through the storm. Storms do not last forever, men. If anything, it will give you a window into the soul of your wife and why she reacts the way she does.

Anger and good sex are both types of passions. One is positive and the other can be negative. Yet together, your relationship can and will survive, but it's going to take work. In essence, the way you respond to your wife when she blows up will only indicate to her how much you are really into the relationship. Will you run like a little boy, or will you stand like a man?

Blessings on all, and remember, real men don't have closets.

Breinigsville, PA USA
23 August 2010
244053BV00001B/2/A